# IT'S NOT TOO LATE

MARGY TRIPP

# IT'S NOT TOO LATE

## Restoring Broken Relationships with Teenage and Adult Children

This book contains wonderful biblical wisdom for parents who yearn for reconciliation with their wayward teens and young adult children.

Parents are called to stop trying to control our prodigals through manipulation and (pharisaic) behaviorism. Instead we must appeal to them with gospel grace and humility, knowing that our parenting works/efforts cannot save them.

We are counseled on how to prepare ourselves spiritually and scripturally before we try to pursue improvement in our relationships with our children.

A great strength of the book is the very specific practical examples of how to humbly seek reconciliation. This will be of great help to parents who don't know where to begin or what to say. I also greatly appreciate the extensive and effective use of Scripture throughout the book.

DR. JIM NEWHEISER: Director of the Christian Counseling Program and Associate Professor of Practical Theology at Reformed Theological Seminary, Charlotte, NC

If you are reading this, you are almost certainly hurting and quite possibly hopeless. Please, let Margy Tripp comfort you and give you biblical hope. I have witnessed the epidemic that has swept our land: children of godly parents who have slammed the door and locked their heartbroken parents out of their lives. That is why I have been waiting for this book. Margy's empathetic wisdom is the key to open your child's rebellious heart and heal your once happy home. Please read it, trust it, apply it; and watch the Holy Spirit work on your children, and you.

TODD FRIEL: Author *Reset for Parents*

As a parent, not many things are more painful than a broken relationship with your teenager or adult child. Margy Tripp, set by step, gives you a path forward, that potentially closes that gap. Not with lectures, but with humility and love. You'll be blessed and encouraged by this book.

PAUL E. MILLER: Executive Director of seeJesus, a global discipleship mission, and author of numerous books and interactive Bible study materials

Building upon firm confidence in the heart-transforming power of the gospel, Margy Tripp brings hope-sustaining help to discouraged and hurting parents. She not only delivers counsel that is biblical, but also practical and wisely applied to the minds and hearts of parents who are wondering if it is too late for them or their family. Learn from the wealth of her wisdom.
PAUL TAUTGES: Author, *Anxiety: Knowing God's Peace,* and many other books; Senior Pastor, Cornerstone Community Church, Mayfield Heights, Ohio; Founder, Counseling One Another

In *It's Not Too Late,* Margy Tripp has written a book that not only is an effective, compassionate, gospel-centered guide to rebuilding relationships with teenage and adult children. It is also a valuable resource for parents to read when their children are young! Reading this book will deepen the hearts of parents to see the wonder of God's wisdom and unlock the power of the gospel to both prevent and heal broken relationships. It should be required reading for all parents. Yes, the wisdom in this book will aid in restoring relationships that may appear to be irretrievable. But, just as valuable is the opportunity to use Margy's biblical insight and wisdom to learn how to avoid brokenness in the first place. *It's Not Too Late* is a must read for any parent who desires to bring the good news of the gospel to the next generation and beyond.
JAY YOUNTS: Author *Everyday Talk* and *When Life Turns Upside Down*

Margy's encouragement in this book is that *it's not too late.* God has an agenda for you. There are things you can do to change the dynamics of your broken relationship with your young adult. This book will take you on a journey. It will deepen your understanding about what happened in your relationship with your son or daughter. It will provide you with the insight needed to initiate new ways to engage your young adult. It will encourage you toward humility and faith for the spiritual battle of moving toward your child in ways that are gracious and gospel centered. It will give you hope as you are reminded that God is at work in all things for your good and his glory.
TEDD TRIPP: Author, Pastor, Conference Speaker
(From *The Foreword*)

It's Not Too Late
Restoring Broken Relationships with
Teenage and Adult Children
Margy Tripp



ISBNS:
978-1-63342-240-7 paper
978-1-63342-241-4 epub
978-1-63342-242-1 mobi



Cover design and typeset by www.greatwriting.org

Printed in the United States of America

Shepherd Press
P.O. Box 24
Wapwallopen, PA 18660
www.shepherdpress.com

# Contents

*This book is dedicated to*

*My precious husband, my greatest earthly teacher, whose biblical theology has prompted me to learn humbling spiritual life lessons from my Heavenly Father.*

*My dear children and their precious spouses and my much-loved grandchildren who have loved my strengths and forgiven my weaknesses.*

# Acknowledgments

*It's Not Too Late* is the fruit of many years of personal contemplation and counseling parents who are in agony over broken relationships with teens and adult children. I am grateful for the honest and self-disclosing conversations with scores of parents whose hearts were desperate for gospel-powered help for their families. They have fueled and refined my thoughts. Many of these parents have encouraged me to write the things they have found transformative for their journey in reconciling with teens and adult children.

Tedd and I have spent countless hours talking about our parenting and relationships with our children over our fifty-three years of marriage. Tedd's preaching and nurture over those years has shaped my responses to trials and grief, as well as to joys and triumphs. He has been my greatest spiritual mentor.

I have also benefitted from remembering my own parents' responses to five lively and sometimes ornery children. Both their love for God and faithful prayer life have influenced my reflections in *It's Not Too Late.*

Friends and co-laborers have also encouraged me. Linda Riggall suggested changing the title from *What If It's Too Late?* to *It's Not Too Late*—a good change. She also gently encouraged me many times to get on with writing.

My son, Aaron, read my early efforts and challenged me to continue to write for the sake of hurting parents and suggested that much of the content is needed for parents to be proactive in establishing and maintaining good relationships with their children.

Jim Holmes has walked me through stages of preparation for publication and has been a wonderful adviser and an encouragement to me.

Above all, I have been entreated by my own heart, and what I believe to be the prompting of the Holy Spirit, to share what God has made precious truth to me. It is hard truth, but freeing truth, to be humbled by God's Spirit at work in us through his Word.

# Foreword

The pain of prodigal sons or daughters is often felt the most keenly by parents who fully invested themselves in intentional parenting. We have spoken with many heartbroken parents who are confused and even a little disappointed in God.

> We did everything we were taught to do. We were always in church; if the doors were open, our family was there. Family worship was a daily priority. We sacrificed to provide a Christian education. Our son won prizes for Scripture memorization. He never gave us any trouble. He even went on mission trips with young people from church. But in college everything changed. He never did get connected to a good church. He started hanging out with young people who were into drugs and the whole party scene. Now he wants nothing to do with Christianity and gets pretty hostile when we bring it up or ask what happened.
>
> Meanwhile we have friends who were worldly Christians, inconsistent in training their kids, allowed them to watch movies we forbid in our home, they attend church spasmodically, sent their kids to public school, they allow their children far more latitude when it came to making choices and you should see their kids. They love God, they are active in church; they are the young adults we always wanted our kids to be.

Heartbroken parents are bewildered and confused. They never expected to face such hostility and anger from their kids. They are at a loss about what to do. How can they get beyond the hostility and anger? How can they disarm the rebellion? The experience of broken relationships with teens or young adults is overwhelming. It casts a shadow over all of life. Family events that should be full of joy become reminders of loss.

Margy's encouragement in this book is that *it's not too late.* God has an agenda for you. There are things you can do to change the dynamics of your broken relationship with your young adult. This book will take you on a journey. It will deepen your understanding about what happened in your relationship with your son or daughter. It will provide you with the insight needed to initiate new ways to engage your young adult. It will encourage you toward humility and faith needed for the spiritual battle of moving toward your child in ways that are gracious and gospel centered. It will give you hope as you are reminded that God is at work in all things for your good and his glory.

The teaching in *It's Not Too Late* flows from our life experience and the things God taught us in developing healthy relationships with our adult children. It is also the fruit of literally hundreds of hours of counseling that Margy has undertaken with suffering parents.

These experiences have left Margy full of hope in the power of the gospel and the goodness of God's capacity to use all the trials of life to refine us and bring us forth as pure gold.

*Tedd Tripp, Author, Pastor, Conference Speaker*

## A Prayer for Parents

*Lord, there are no doubt moms and dads reading this who have felt the pain and anguish of children who are angry and bitter toward them and who have forsaken their Christian heritage.*

*Psalm 34 reminds us, "The LORD is near to the brokenhearted and saves the crushed in spirit." You are a loving heavenly Father and you are sympathetic to all of our needs. You comfort your people, and you give everything needed in the difficult trials of life.*

*But you haven't stopped there. You've given us instruction. You've given us direction in your Word. You've helped us to understand, not only how we can know you in the midst of grief and regret but how to approach the ministry of reconciliation.*

*We pray that as we look at these difficult issues, you will draw near to us by your Spirit; that your Spirit will minister comfort and hope to our hurting souls.*

*We thank you for Christ's sake,*
*Amen.*

# 1

# *It's Not Too Late!*

Why are we tempted to feel like "it's too late"? Perhaps it is your child's age—he is a teen now or even an adult. Perhaps it is the degree of brokenness in your relationship—it feels like there is no hope for reconciliation. Perhaps it is the sense you have of your child's rejection of spiritual things, and even rejection of God or the Christian faith. Here is important truth for you to consider as those thoughts crowd your mind and heart. It is *always* God's work of grace that subdues rebellious hearts. That's what happened to you and me. It is God's Spirit who brings us, and our children, to repentance and faith—not our works or our children's works.

Ephesians 2:8–9 reminds us that ". . . *by grace you have been saved through faith. And this is not your own doing; it is the gift of God, not a result of works, so that no one may boast.*" It is by grace alone that *we* are saved. That is true for our children, too.

It is God's Spirit who brings spiritual life to us and to our children. But fear is a great spiritual struggle for parents. We can fall into deep and desperate child-rearing chasms out of fear. We fear that our children will make bad decisions, develop bad habits and relationships, and not choose Christianity over the world and its pleasures. We might then fall into a parenting role that denies the gospel. It feels like we must somehow make enough rules to keep them safe. We must create incentives and disincentives to ensure their spiritual well-being.

Rules and incentives are valid and appropriate in their place. But we can become so dependent on these external mechanisms that prayer and hope in Christ are forgotten. This is when we are most likely to become distressed over our children, and give in to anger and manipulation—all of which destroy relationships. This dependence on our own efforts in parenting also leaves us hopeless and faithless. Parents search their memories to try to find the point at which they failed. It might sound like this.

"Where did we go wrong?"
"How could this happen when we tried so hard?"
"What about God's promises?"
"I have racked my brain to try to think where I failed!"

We have to get our parenting expectations in line with God's saving agenda. Think of it this way. The parents' role resembles that of the farmer cultivating the heart, planting seeds of truth and tending the heart, and then trusting God for the harvest.

Deuteronomy 6 is wonderfully descriptive of the parenting role. Verses 6–9 frame the daily instruction parents are to give their children in God's ways.

> These commandments that I give you today are to be on your hearts. Impress them on your children. Talk about them when you sit at home and when you walk along the road, when you lie down and when you get up. Tie them as symbols on your hands and bind them on your foreheads. Write them on the doorframes of your houses and on your gates. (Deuteronomy 6:6–9, NIV)

Notice that the parents' role is that of instruction. The instruction is heartfelt. *These commandments that I give you today are to be on your hearts.*

We cannot impress our children with the beauty and symmetry of God's direction for our lives unless we have been moved by the beauty and suitability of God's law for our own lives. Legalistic application of God's law in our own Christian experience will ring like a cracked bell in our children's ears. They will resist God's law as restrictive and oppressive.

Think about the word "impress" in verse 7. It carries a sense of my child's need for God's law, but also our mode of communicating. It is a positive rather than a negative term. We could use the word "influence" just as readily to describe the task of graciously drawing children into the beauty and appropriateness of living in God's world in God's way.

The instruction is a consistent and winsome daily presence in family life. The entire day is framed by gracious and godly instruction: sitting, walking, waking, resting. And God's revelation is always before us, directing and interpreting our experience of life. This is the force of God's law being written on our doorframes and gates. It is a hallmark—a presence that characterizes all that is said and done. Our homes should reflect consideration of God's ways so that the freedom of the gospel of grace is always before the family. The graces of Christian living are these: unconditional love, joy, peace, patience, kindness, goodness, faithfulness, gentleness, self-control (Galatians 5:22–26), humility, forgiveness, sacrifice, thanksgiving, forbearance, honesty, trust, hopefulness, perseverance (1 Corinthians 13:4–8a), generosity and consideration in speech, loyalty to God and others (whether they are friend or foe, Ephesians 4:29–32), hospitality, orderliness, predictability that brings security, and rejoicing. All of these, and more, will mark the conversation and demeanor of our homes.

Verses 20 - 25 of Deuteronomy 6 are a godly apologetic for the choices parents have made to honor God's law when children ask questions such as: "Why do we always have to go to church?" or "Why is our family different from other families?" We are not different because of social status, money, poverty, heritage, education, skills, intelligence, or opportunities. We are different because of who God is and what God has done! When we appeal to any of the above descriptors to motivate our children to know God or walk in his ways, or to explain why we are different from the culture around us, we are either appealing to pride or avarice to reason with them. Deuteronomy 6 answers the questions with power and clarity!

> "When your son asks you in time to come, 'What is the meaning of the testimonies and the statutes and the rules that the LORD our God has commanded you?' then you shall say to your son, 'We were Pharaoh's slaves in Egypt. And the LORD brought us out of Egypt with a mighty hand. And the LORD showed signs and wonders, great and grievous, against Egypt and against Pharaoh and all his household, before our eyes. And he brought us out from there, that he might bring us in and give us the land that he swore to give to our fathers. And the Lord commanded us to do all these statutes, to fear the LORD our God, for our good always, that he might preserve us alive, as we are this day. And it will be righteousness for us, if we are careful to do all this commandment before the LORD our God, as he has commanded us.'"
> (Deuteronomy 6:20–25)

What precious words these are! Rather than answering our teens' complaints about family choices to follow God with, "Because I said so!" or by reasoning with them that it is because of social status, money, poverty, heritage, education, skills, intelligence, or opportunities, we can bring them the gospel. We can answer: "We were lost and enslaved in our sin. Anger, bitterness, emptiness, lawlessness, and purposelessness ruled our lives. But God mercifully redeemed us from our sin and set us free to know fulfillment of life in him. We are able to live consistently with our Creator's purpose for us—to bring glory to him and to serve Christ's Kingdom by loving others. We don't do this perfectly, we know, but purposefully by the grace given to us through the perfect life, atoning death, and resurrection of our Savior, Jesus Christ. In fact, he is our High Priest who is always interceding for us at the right hand of God. Since this is our testimony, why would we not organize our life and family around God's calling to live for him?"

This is a glorious response to a complaining, rebellious, ornery teen! Any other answer will come back to bite us when our children either learn to live in light of the worldly motivations we have used or reject the worldly motivations we have used.

Psalm 145:4 describes the parent's task as well. *"One generation shall commend your works to another, and shall declare your mighty acts."* That is the calling of parents, to commend God's works to the next generation. Psalm 145 goes on to describe whole categories of instruction: God's works, acts, majesty, power, deeds, and all his attributes. Psalm 145 recommends many forms of instruction: commend, tell, speak, meditate, proclaim, celebrate, and sing. So, the parents' role is to instruct with passion and conviction and pray with hope and confidence. That is where the parents' role ends. Salvation is of the Lord. If you think about it seriously, you would not want your child's salvation to depend on your parenting. None of us could perform well enough to secure our child's eternal well-being. Our resolve is often inconsistent and our spiritual fervor waxes and wanes. Our insights into God's ways and truth are finite. Praise God we can bank on something more powerful than our performance! In fact, God's resolve is sovereign and complete. Consider Christ's teaching in John's Gospel about the Good Shepherd.

> Jesus answered them, "I told you, and you do not believe. The works that I do in my Father's name bear witness about me, but you do not believe because you are not among my sheep. My sheep hear my voice, and I know them, and they follow me. I give them eternal life, and they will never perish, and no one will snatch them out of my hand. My Father, who has given them to me, is greater than all, and no one is able to snatch them out of the Father's hand. I and the Father are one."
> (John 10:25–30)

This brings us back to our farming analogy. The success of the harvest is never to the credit of the farmer. The farmer depends on "the Lord of the harvest" for the fruit of his labors. Godly nurture always provides the best shaping influences in our children's lives. We would not deny that for a moment. We always want to provide godly shaping influences, but neither our successes nor our failures (as spiritual farmers) are the deciding factor in the harvest—that is, in our children's response to God. Just as the farmer looks to God for the bounty of the harvest, so the parents pray for God's Spirit to bring his truth to life in the hearts of their children. The parents' role is that of the farmer cultivating the heart, planting seeds of truth, and tending the heart. The harvest is the work of God's Spirit. We all stand before God responsible for the choices that we make. This is true for our children as well.

Parents need to be reminded of this truth. It keeps us from placing inordinate hope in our parenting methods and choices. It keeps us from undue self-recrimination when we fail. It frees us to have humility to acknowledge our sin and our need for God's help to our spouse and our children. It clears the way for appropriate self-evaluation. It discourages harsh judgment of the parenting methods and choices of others, and it discourages pride over our seeming success. Often it is the parents who strive the most diligently who are the most disappointed in God, or themselves, or their children, when their children reject Christian faith. This drives us to our knees in prayer for God's saving mercy and grace in the lives of our children.

Think about your parenting experience. You have heard the

call in Scripture to shepherd your children in the nurture and admonition of the Lord You may wonder why you did not hear these things years ago. But wherever you are now, God calls you to take hold of the plow. When and where you heard biblical truth about child-rearing must be left to God's sovereign purposes. Start now to shepherd your child's heart, regardless of your child's age! The apostle Paul instructs us to respond to opposition, guiding the Lord's servant to

> . . . [correct] his opponents with gentleness. God may perhaps grant them repentance leading to a knowledge of the truth, and they may come to their senses and escape from the snare of the devil, after being captured by him to do his will.
> (2 Timothy 2:25–26)

But how can we hope to "plow up" or soften hearts that have already become hard? Our children harden their hearts toward God just as they harden their hearts toward us. Perhaps you are among the scores of Christian parents whose children professed faith in Christ, but now you find that you live with unresolved brokenness in your relationships.

How can we begin this restoration? That's where the following chapters will lead us. It will be a process. Remember, relationships were not damaged over a brief time or series of events; the damage happened over years. Reconciliation will take time to initiate and implement. We must learn how to disarm rebellion. This is a spiritual journey in which we remove our child's sense of justification for rebelling against us so that he is left only with resistance to God. Then the power and grace of the gospel can invade the heart—the seat of rebellion.

This is serious work. When children have strayed from home, either figuratively or literally, parents suffer agony and grief just under the surface of everyday life. You may have read this chapter and felt that this doesn't describe your circumstances exactly. But hear me out before you conclude that this book is about other people's relationship struggles with their teen or adult child. Allow the overall truth to guide your conclusions. The specific details and illustrations may not exactly fit your experience, but God's Word holds gospel-powered reconciliation for renewing and healing broken relationships.

I know that the thoughts I am sharing with you will be challenging and may be very painful for you to read and consider. But I want to encourage you that I am speaking to you from firsthand experience. I have learned these difficult spiritual lessons, so I do not bring them to you lightly or thoughtlessly. I have experienced them myself, first as a rebellious teen and later as a mother. Reconciliation and healing in your relationship with your rebellious child will always be humbling—but God has promised in his Word that he gives grace to the humble—that he brings beauty from ashes when we are willing to humble ourselves before him, and that he will lift us up.

*It's Not Too Late!*

# 2

# *How Did This Happen?*

The phone rang in the late afternoon. An anxious mother described a fifteen-year-old son whose rebellion and disrespect to her and his father were over the top. He had become violent in his speech and had even damaged the doors and walls of his room in fits of rage against parental discipline. This weary mother asked if I could help with intervention for their son. I agreed to talk further with them.

Many heartbroken parents grow discouraged and disheartened when their children show signs of rebellion. They conclude, "It's too late to shepherd my children! We lost control years ago!"

Perhaps Christian parents realize that the early opportunities to shepherd their children were lost because of the way they lived before they came to faith in Christ. So, poor habits of life interfered with applying biblical truth to their parenting. Or perhaps parents lacked understanding of God's ways. So, parents were not thinking in biblical terms about nurture, motivation, correction, and discipline when their children were young. For some parents, the circumstances of life may have interfered with the nurturing process—for example, the death of a spouse, lost jobs, a broken marriage, moves, illness, or divorce and remarriage.

The fruit of all these is painful! Relationships are suffering or broken with children and teens. Regular confrontations with rebellious children have led to escalating hurtful language on both sides. Parents feel wounded by their children's biting words. Parents feel defensive and accuse children of disrespect and not loving or caring about the family. Conversation becomes increasingly difficult. Parents and children cannot get past the most recent verbal barrage that felt like a stab in the back. The emotional stress of a deteriorating relationship sometimes even overwhelms the agony of rebellious behavior. A vicious cycle of accusations, hurt, pain, and ugly responses ensues. Tears, sadness, sleeplessness, and solitude shape a family atmosphere that is heavy with suspicion, disrespect, avoidance, and occasional temper eruptions. Weary parents take the hurts personally. They live daily on an emotional roller coaster driven by their own guilt and regrets and anger over their child's rebellion.

So, parents fear that it is "too late" to shepherd their teen's heart! Every day is filled with the parents' desperate efforts to warn and constrain their teen's disrespectful, disobedient, destructive behavior and attitudes. Home has become a war zone. Mom is frazzled from dealing with it. Dad feels helpless. Both parents are losing patience and even find it hard to love this kid. The more they try to get things under control, the more resentful their teen becomes. Everyone is taking sides. Parents find their own relationship strained. They blame each other for the dilemma. They feel confused. They don't know how to bring any resolution to this situation with their hardened and cynical teenager. Fearing that their authority is ebbing away, parents get louder and more demanding. They threaten with more onerous punishments to hold on to power. At the same time, they are filled with doubt and dread. "What will happen to this teen?" "Who can help?" "How will they 'turn out'?" "It's all my fault!" "How could this happen when we have always attended church?" "What will people think of us?" These tormenting thoughts and questions only fuel the angst parents struggle with every day.

Single parents poignantly feel the agony of broken relationship with rebellious children. Fear, doubt, regret, loneliness, and hopelessness fill the hours between confrontations with their children. They blame themselves and their life circumstances. "If only I had help!" "I can't go on." "I just want to give up." "What hope is there for someone like me?"

Some parents are in the even more complicated waters of having adult children living at home who have rejected the parents' values and lifestyle, leading to tension and broken relationships. Such adult children have a sense of independence due to their age and may have even lived on their own for some time in college or work circumstances away from home, but now have returned to their parents' home.

These parents have the added struggle of maintaining an appropriate atmosphere in their home, but also navigating the troubled waters of another adult who feels entitled to live as an independent person in the family unit. This creates obvious tensions. The adult child doesn't want to be treated like a teen, and the parents have great difficulty keeping any semblance of order in their home with one of the family members not participating in family life. Soon tempers flare and feelings are hurt. Each faction begins to draw the battle lines and is unwilling to hear and understand the other. Or on the other end of the continuum, parents can be afraid of appropriate confrontation with their young adult for fear of further brokenness in the family relationships. Parents resort to emotional distancing, the silent treatment and disapproving looks and snide comments to register their frustration. This only stiffens their child's resolve to resist.

For some parents, children have grown into adulthood, left home, and left behind a broken relationship with one or both parents. Their broken relationship is not on the surface because they are not confronted with it daily, but parents grieve over the brokenness and loss of extended family relationships. Parents fear to reach out to resolve the breach because they fear rejection. "Anything I say or do will only make things worse. We always end up fighting," they say. If their children are too busy with their new life elsewhere, and have regrets or hurts over the broken relationship with their parents, they generally avoid reconciliation, thinking something like this: "Some things never change. I'll find my happiness, acceptance, and fulfillment in new relationships or circumstances."

Parents of adult children carry a weight of guilt and regret mixed with defensiveness and justification for their parenting methods. These parents often struggle with bitterness over the hurts they have suffered at the hands of their children. They are devastated at the disloyalty of their children. They are tempted to harden their hearts against their offspring in order to stave off the terrible daily agony from the acrimonious breakdown with one or more of their adult children.

## *THE MOST COMMON REASON FOR BROKEN RELATIONSHIPS*

There is more than one explanation for broken relationships between parents and children. Sometimes the most diligent and careful parenting cannot curb the rebellious bent of a child's heart. But the most common reason for broken relationships between parents and children may surprise you.

As Tedd and I have taught the "Shepherding a Child's Heart" and "Instructing a Child's Heart" material around the world, we have learned that there is one primary reason for this breakdown. It is this. Parents have sometimes mixed loving God and striving to do the right thing with their own struggles—like anger or a legalistic view of the Christian faith—and that has created an atmosphere in which rebellion can grow. None of that excuses the rebellion, but family life has produced conditions in which the rebellion of the child's heart has taken root. The Word of God reminds and warns that parents can be a stumbling block to children.

> Fathers, do not provoke your children to anger, but bring them up in the discipline and instruction of the Lord. (Ephesians 6:4)

When parents use the law of God to instruct, warn, motivate, and encourage their child to do what is good or to refrain from what is wrong, but then respond to the child's failure in ungodly ways, the child will resist.

Here is our problem. Often parents forge ahead with the Bible in one hand and the parenting methods of their parents or the "experts" in the other hand. There are two problems with this. The *first* problem is simply that biblical parenting does not integrate with other parenting methods. Here's why. The Bible is clear and exclusive regarding instruction, motivation, nurture, correction, and discipline. There is no need to borrow from other methods to fill in the gaps. Doing so creates a disjointed presentation to our children, which leaves them confused and uncertain of the parents' agenda. Let me illustrate.

We use God's law, the standards of the Bible, to establish the rules for our home. But when our child fails to keep the rules, we might turn to the familiar tactics of our own youth, or some behavioristic punishment to bring change in behavior rather than communicating the clear instruction of the Bible. It might sound like this:

"When I was your age, if I lied to my dad, I would have been tanned within an inch of my life. You better straighten up and fly right if you value your backside!"

Another might be: "From now on you will be fined a dollar for every bad word that comes out of your mouth! I'll teach you to get rid of nasty language!"

Of course, lying and bad language are censured by God's Word, but these parental solutions focus on merely changing external behavior. The child's heart motivation is not addressed. Even if the parents can manage to change the child's behavior through threats, the child's character and conscience are never touched. This is called *behaviorism.* Behaviorism is the management of behavior through incentives and disincentives. Behaviorism is concerned with external behavior rather than character. Behaviorism denies the life-giving message of the gospel in response to our children's temptation to sin. God's agenda is not to frighten or threaten his people. God's Word is clear about consequences, and even in bringing chastisement, God's agenda is restoration. Consequences play a role in the nurture, instruction, and motivation of our children, but God does not intend consequences to be the reason for change. Consequences only illustrate, both positively and negatively, God's agenda to change hearts. When hearts are changed by the gospel, behavior follows.

The *second* problem is following the experts of the world. There are scores of parenting paradigms abroad in social media, magazines, and books. Once again, parents may use God's Word to establish the standards of conduct for their home. But then those same parents often try the experts' methods, moving from one to another, or even mixing various elements of several methods to motivate and correct their children. Everything from "tough love" to parent-child contracts litter the daily experience of some children and teens. When one method doesn't prove effective, parents often turn to another. The effect of this parenting hodgepodge leaves children confused, frustrated, and with a growing sense of injustice. This creates a hothouse for a rebellious heart.

The most popular parenting model is behaviorism—the carrot and the stick—where people have either promised rewards and prizes to secure their children's good behavior, or they have threatened punishments, using authoritarian control, or manipulation, or guilt and fear, to ensure their children's good behavior. Children raised with secular motivators, especially when mixed with a form of Christian values, are often sullen, bitter, and rebellious because they feel manipulated. Other children learn to keep the external rules and they become proud and arrogant. They are like the Pharisees that Christ continually admonishes in the Gospels because they mistake their legalistic law-keeping for righteousness.

Of course, many Christian parents have striven to use biblical methods of parenting, but often even biblical methods are corrupted with sin—with anger, selfish motives, laziness (because it's such hard work) or inconsistency. One day we're spot on, but the next day we just don't see the same behavior as that important.

This corruption of God's ways may result from not knowing God's ways—simply not being taught how to lead our children according to the Bible. But even when God's truth is known and loved, there is, for all of us, the struggle with indwelling sin that crops up in the process of parenting, undermining our effectiveness. Parents must be quick to repent, seek forgiveness, and be restored when they have failed. Otherwise, their children will become hardened to parental instruction and discipline. Even when they comply in early childhood, they are hardening their hearts toward the day when their hurts and sense of injustice will be expressed—generally in their adolescent to teen years, or, for some more reticent personalities, when they are adults!

If any of these descriptions of children's behavior or your parenting is true in your home, take heart. I want to encourage you that it is not too late! Let's get started down the path to reconciliation.

# 3

# *Disarming Rebellion*

Christian parents long to have their children trust God for the spiritual strength to obey, whether they are twelve or twenty-two. So far, so good. But, as we have already noted, when parents use behaviorism and manipulation to motivate their children, whether by using positive rewards or negative punishments, children come to feel justified in their resistance and rebellion. Here's why. Christian faith and behaviorism don't mix! Children feel confused, perhaps even sinned against.

Tedd and I were having lunch at a conference with leaders whose lives were largely consumed with the spiritual and academic education of their children. As we talked, we listened to accounts of heartbreak with teenage and grown children who had rejected parental authority and the Christian faith. Further discussion began to unearth this tragic juxtaposition of behaviorism and Christian truth in Christian homes.

## *UNDERSTAND THE RESISTANCE*

How can we disarm this sense of justification our children have against our spiritual leadership? How did our children become armed against us? Let's begin by understanding how our children get into the state of rebellion and what our role is to assist in their release. It is important for us to understand the source of resistance.

Let me suggest two foundational strategies for understanding your child's resistance. This must be clear in your mind before you begin this process. Don't look for how to change your children; think rather about how *you* need to change! Disarming your child's rebellion starts with you, not with them!

It is tempting to put it at their doorstep, but it has to start with you. You will begin to understand their resistance as you consider the following:

## 1.
## *Think Clearly about Your Own View of God's Instruction and Discipline of You as His Child*

You cannot make corrections in your relationship with your children until your own heart has been plowed up. A big snare to godly parenting exists long before parents ever instruct and correct their first child. That snare is a mistaken view of God and his purposes in instructing and disciplining us! We are mistaken when we believe that God thinks and acts like we do as fallen people.

The view of God and his purposes we believe and practice in the stuff of everyday life *is* the one we will teach and practice on our children! Our model for instruction, discipline, correction, and motivation of our children will imitate our view of God and his treatment of us. Romans 12:2 illustrates the danger we're in. It is possible for us to be taken in by the mindset of the world—to follow the advice and counsel of unbelievers. Paul counsels us to allow the Scriptures and the ministry of God's Spirit to transform and maintain a renewed mind—a mind that is shaped by Scripture and the ministry of the Holy Spirit and is consistent with God's callings and provision in Christ. A renewed mind alters our perception and therefore our practice. Having renewed minds enables us *"test and approve what God's will is—his good, pleasing and perfect will."* (Romans 12:2, NIV).

God's law and the gospel of grace are suited to the condition of fallen people. An accurate view of God's purpose toward us must precede bringing instruction and discipline to our children that they can receive and believe.

We need to begin our journey to disarm rebellion by understanding the difference between behavioristic instruction and discipline *and* biblical instruction and discipline. The ways they are incompatible will become apparent.

*Behavioristic Instruction*
In behaviorism, parental instruction exists to facilitate the parents' personal agenda and gratification. Success, power, desires, lusts, dreams, and hopes are the agenda; personal peace, prosperity, ease, convenience, and recognition are the gratification. In our culture, instruction and discipline exist primarily for selfish purposes. Instruction exists to bring about success. Discipline exists to make others conform to our wishes. I am not suggesting that parents who use behaviorism do not love and want what is best for their children. However, I am suggesting that behaviorism serves the general philosophy of secular culture—that success can be measured by the coins of value in the culture—personal peace, prosperity, ease, convenience, and recognition.

*Behavioristic Discipline*
Discipline, in behaviorism, is simply a system of rewards and punishments that appeal enough to be a motivator or sting enough to be a deterrent in achieving our goals. Our secular culture uses rewards and punishments unashamedly and successfully. "Be on your best behavior. I don't want you embarrassing me!" "If you're 'good,' I'll buy you. . ." or "You better. . . or you'll pay!" "If you're smart, you'll do what you must to get. . ." or "I'm the boss. If you mess up, I'll get you!"

Children become armed against ungodly methods of constraining and controlling them. This is particularly true where Christian faith and behaviorism have been mixed together, wittingly or unwittingly, to keep control. Parents may perceive their children's resistance as resistance to God and Christian faith. However, what they observe may be resistance to unholy methods of discipline and correction.

If you think about it, that's a struggle we all have, isn't it? When we feel sinned against, we have a sense of justification that grows up inside us. So, we may have an internal response that scoffs, "I'll never trust them again," or we may have an external response that either tells them off or determines to avoid the person or people who have hurt us. This often produces broken relationships that lead to bitterness where we promise, "I'm staying away from them—they're dangerous people." We are all tempted to respond to hurts and wrongs in these ways.

Our children grow the same sense of justification when they feel we have sinned against them. Proverbs 18:19 states that *"a brother offended is more unyielding than a strong city."*

Parents tell their children that the gospel is the only help for our struggles with sinful responses. That's good theology. The gospel *is* the only help for our struggle with sin. But parents' behavioristic manipulation of their children denies the gospel, and the children become armed against their parents. Picture them with weapons! They become armed against this double standard. They feel justified in their rebellion.

What does it mean to deny the gospel? When parents' hope of change consists of the rewards and punishments of behaviorism rather than the power of grace, the gospel is missing. When parents are satisfied with external behavioral change that is motivated by rewards and punishments rather than conviction of sin and the mercy and enablement of Christ, the gospel is missing. Children conclude two things: First, external behavior is what Christian faith is about, and secondly, that Christian faith and grace are not the remedy for sin—instead, rewards and punishments are. This also dictates a false view of God's agenda, which we will consider later.

So, children may *experience* scores of motivators from parents that deny the grace and hope of the gospel. They will then increasingly resist the parents and the parents' methods. They resist the message and the messenger. The gospel becomes a casualty!

In a counseling session, hurting parents were describing their family devotion times to illustrate their teen's rebellion. Father's habit was to pray first for the biggest sinner each day down to the least disobedient, which, of course, highlighted this teen's failures daily as the sinner at the top of the prayer list. In rebellion mixed with hurt, the teen sat with back turned and arms crossed through mandatory family worship. We looked together at Luke 6:42. God calls us to humbly acknowledge personal sin before bringing the sin of others to light. After being moved by God's Word, the father began praying for himself at the top of the list and displayed grace and compassion toward the teen's struggles. In response to the father's humility, even though it was only a beginning, the teen turned around and displayed less contempt for family worship. Children will resist the parents and the parents' message when it disfigures God's marvelous grace-filled agenda.

Scores of parents have said to me, "I don't know what happened. I thought everything was good with raising my children. Then, all of a sudden, it was as if I didn't know them. They began to be disrespectful, insolent, disobedient—just rebellious! What's wrong with my teenager? And how can I fix it?" Other parents confess that their child seemed to be born with his fist in the air! Still other family relationships seem to disintegrate when the children leave home and establish a family of their own. Of course, the temptation here is to attribute relationship struggles to our child's new associations—spouse, work colleagues or friends. Parents who fall to this temptation create even deeper brokenness with their children because of their child's newly formed relationship loyalties. Believe it or not—this is at the heart of all the in-law jokes!

As children grow from their very dependent and credulous young years into childhood and then into adolescence and puberty to young adulthood, they are exposed to the effects of sin on life—both their own sin and the sin of others against them. If they allow resentment and bitterness to grow in their heart as it becomes devastated by that sin, their painful experiences, and the circumstances of life in a fallen world, the result will be rebellion, anger, and bitterness. Every heart is faced with this dilemma. How will I interpret and respond to life in a fallen world? Sadly, where resentment, anger, and bitterness set in, that heart becomes its own worst enemy. The sad reality is that anger, resentment, and bitterness destroy the heart of its host. The soul becomes brittle and hardened to the ministries of the fruit of the Spirit—love, joy, peace, patience, kindness, goodness, gentleness, faithfulness, and self-control. Take stock of your own heart. Has the brokenness of the world around you and your own sense of loss left you cynical and harsh in your outlook? Have you become hopeless and sure that there is no help for the future? It is the fruit of bitterness.

These are hearts that need the plowing, cultivating, and

sowing of God's truth in God's way. I call this process of plowing up the hard hearts of children and teens, and even adult children, "disarming rebellion."

*Biblical Instruction*
In stark contrast, all of God's instruction reveals his glory and holiness to the end that we will live for him and worship him in awe and be satisfied and fulfilled in our roles, even in the face of our own failures and the failures of others toward us. God's goal is that we live with a biblical sense of well-being that is driven by faith rather than simply responding emotionally to the people and circumstances of life.

The words of Jesus recorded in Matthew 6:19–34 contrast the goals and gratification of the world with those of God.

> "Do not lay up for yourselves treasures on earth, where moth and rust destroy and where thieves break in and steal, but lay up for yourselves treasures in heaven, where neither moth nor rust destroys and where thieves do not break in and steal. For where your treasure is, there your heart will be also.
>
> "The eye is the lamp of the body. So, if your eye is healthy, your whole body will be full of light, but if your eye is bad, your whole body will be full of darkness. If then the light in you is darkness, how great is the darkness!
>
> "No one can serve two masters, for either he will hate the one and love the other, or he will be devoted to the one and despise the other. You cannot serve God and money.
>
> "Therefore I tell you, do not be anxious about your life, what you will eat or what you will drink, nor about your body, what you will put on. Is not life more than food, and the body more than clothing? Look at the birds of the air: they neither sow nor reap nor gather into barns, and yet your heavenly Father feeds them. Are you not of more value than they? And which of you by being anxious can add a single hour to his span of life? And why are you anxious about clothing? Consider the lilies of the field, how they grow: they neither toil nor spin, yet I tell you, even Solomon in all his

> glory was not arrayed like one of these. But if God so clothes the grass of the field, which today is alive and tomorrow is thrown into the oven, will he not much more clothe you, O you of little faith? Therefore do not be anxious, saying, 'What shall we eat?' or 'What shall we drink?' or 'What shall we wear?' For the Gentiles seek after all these things, and your heavenly Father knows that you need them all. But seek first the kingdom of God and his righteousness, and all these things will be added to you.
>
> "Therefore do not be anxious about tomorrow, for tomorrow will be anxious for itself. Sufficient for the day is its own trouble."
>
> (Matthew 6:19–34)

Christ's teaching in these verses is crowned with: "*But seek first the kingdom of God and his righteousness, and all these things will be added to you*" What gratification!

Trust in God for your sense of well-being. Be content with his purposes for you and his direction. God says that our significance is found in fulfilling the greatest commandment. *"You shall love the Lord your God with all your heart and with all your soul and with all your mind. . You shall love your neighbor as yourself."* Matthew 22:37–40. This is godly instruction toward worthy goals. God's instruction of us is perfectly satisfying.

Parental instruction must focus on God's glory rather than our personal agenda. Rather than emphasizing my agenda for the day as I talk with my children, I could say: "Children, we are representing a glorious God today. He has sacrificed his Son for our redemption. Let's pray for his strength to let our light shine in this dark world." (See Matthew 5:14–16.)

***Biblical Discipline***

How often have you felt that God might be angry with you—that he might not be able to accept you back, yet again, after you have failed? Or perhaps you believe that God hasn't answered your prayers because you have failed? That is not what God is like! That's what fallen human beings are like. Hebrews 12:5–12 describes God's discipline of us.

> And have you forgotten the exhortation that addresses you as sons?
> "My son, do not regard lightly the discipline of the Lord,
> nor be weary when reproved by him.
> For the Lord disciplines the one he loves,
> and chastises every son whom he receives."
> (Hebrews 12:5, 6)

God's *discipline* of his children is to make us holy—to conform us to the image of his Son, our Elder Brother, Christ. God's law has been given to direct our behavior for his glory and our good. When we fail, he is not mad at us. Even when we must reap what we have sown, it only underscores the goodness of God, the wisdom of his truth, and the sadness and destruction of sin.

Do you see relationship with God as grace based or merit based? Do you reason like this? "Oh no, I didn't read my Bible today! So, how can I ask God to help me with this problem?" Or we might find that we have a self-generated sense of confidence as we approach the throne of grace in prayer because we remembered to have personal devotions, rather than because of Christ's finished redemptive work in our behalf. We live and respond to life out of which way we think of God.

How do you think of God's instruction and discipline of you? God's discipline is not selfish. God doesn't burden you with his law and then, for his amusement, make you pay when you fail! Do you see God's standards as a burdensome standard that you must somehow achieve in order to please God and to assure that all will go well for you? And what place do consequences and guilt have in the practical outworking of your theology? Do they serve merely as a deterrent to sin and a way to do penance *or* are consequences and conviction merciful and timely reminders of your need of a Savior and a goad to flee to the cross once again to find mercy and grace in your time of need?

Christ is our model. We are his representatives to our children of the power and grace of the gospel.

Romans 7:21–25 describes Christ as God's gift to rescue us from spiritual death.

> So I find it to be a law that when I want to do right, evil lies close at hand. For I delight in the law of God, in my inner being, but I see in my members another law waging war against the law of my mind and making me captive to the law of sin that dwells in my members. Wretched man that I am! Who will deliver me from this body of death? Thanks be to God through Jesus Christ our Lord!
> (Romans 7:21–25a)

Be careful! It is easy to give assent to the free grace of the gospel as the remedy for our struggles with sin, but to live with anxiety, frustration, fear, and guilt over our sin. Anxiety, frustration, fear and guilt are a tacit denial of the gospel! Of course, our real belief concerning the gospel is exposed by how we respond to the sins of others! Their failures will either drive us to judge and condemn them, or to pray for and encourage them as we hope for the power of Christ's work in them. Our response to our own sins and the sins of others discloses our view of God and his purposes in redemption and sanctification. We cannot cooperate with God's agenda for us in sanctification when we are tethered to our own efforts without reference to the gospel.

We need to repent of any view of God we have that does not recognize his purpose to save, to enable, and to preserve all who put their trust in him. Is this the way you think of God when you fail? Which description of instruction and discipline do you practice? You see, whatever view you have of a relationship with God when *you* fail *is* what you will both pass on to your children *and* it is the foundation of instruction and discipline you will practice with your children. That *is* the view of God you will give your children of God's instruction and discipline of them.

Identify the ways you view God and his response to you in your everyday struggles. What you believe about God has shaped the view of God you have presented to your children. Repent of any view of God that denies his purpose to save, enable, and preserve all who put their trust in him, even those who have sinned against you.

Purpose to have your daily life exude that hope before your children. Focus on redemption. Obviously, you have to identify your child's sin, but focus on redemption. Nowhere in God's Word does it say, "I just want you to stay in that muddle, in that slough of despond for a while, because I want you to pay for your sin." No, God uses his Word to convict us of sin, to show us our sin. Why? So that we may take our vision off of ourselves and put it on the cross. We must do that for our children too.

Psalm 103 is such a picture of this truth for us.

> Bless the LORD, O my soul,
> and forget not all his benefits,
> who forgives all your iniquity,
> who heals all your diseases,
> who redeems your life from the pit,
> who crowns you with steadfast love and mercy. . .
> The LORD is merciful and gracious,
> slow to anger and abounding in steadfast love.
> He will not always chide,
> nor will he keep his anger forever.
> He does not deal with us according to our sins,
> nor repay us according to our iniquities.
> For as high as the heavens are above the earth,
> so great is his steadfast love toward those who fear him;
> as far as the east is from the west,
> so far does he remove our transgressions from us.
> As a father shows compassion to his children,
> so the LORD shows compassion to those who fear him.
> For he knows our frame;
> he remembers that we are dust.
> (Psalm 103:2–14)

## 2.
## *Recognize That You Are a Tangible Representative of the Unseen God to Your Children*

This is obvious but, oh, so hard to apply! In Hebrews 12, the writer presents a compelling argument for parents as representatives of God as he uses the father's role to illustrate his discipline of us.

> It is for discipline that you have to endure. God is treating you as sons. For what son is there whom his father does not discipline? If you are left without discipline, in which all have participated, then you are illegitimate children and not sons. Besides this, we have had earthly fathers who disciplined us and we respected them. Shall we not much more be subject to the Father of spirits and live? For they disciplined us for a short time as it seemed best to them, but he disciplines us for our good, that we may share his holiness. (Hebrews 12:7–10)

We want to acknowledge that we are representatives of this unseen God. We want our children to know that it is our purpose and our desire—even though we sometimes fail—to represent God in the beauty of who he is. We want them to know he is the judge, but we also want them to know that, because of the work of the Lord Jesus Christ, he is a gracious and loving Heavenly Father. Tell them, "That's what I want to be like." You can pray, and ask your teenagers to pray that you will accurately represent this Heavenly Father.

Because you are a tangible representative of the unseen God, children, from their earliest memory through their teenage years, increasingly attribute to God the treatment received from the hands of parents. Very young children accept unquestioningly your assertions about this God whom they cannot see or hear. Their experience of God consists mainly in your experience of God. When you tell a young child that he can trust God in a particular circumstance, he will generally be quieted and reassured because you are the primary source of calming reassurance to him that all will be okay. As children shed their credulity, their personal opinions and assessments replace unquestioning belief in the unseen God. But God continues to bear the reputation formed by your parenting.

Harsh, legalistic, ungracious, or manipulative treatment from us causes our teenagers to resist God's authority. Then they will also resist our attempts, as agents of this God, to discipline and direct them. Oh, if we could only remember that every time we're tempted to allow angry words to escape our lips! We give God a reputation. When we sin against our children, they resist God's authority.

Gentle, merciful, gracious, understanding and nurturing treatment from parents leaves teenagers open and accepting of God's authority and our attempts as agents of God to influence and direct them. Your children get their sense of what God is like from the people who say they are God's children, because children imitate their parents. You see, we want to live like our Heavenly Father in our homes in such a way that God has a good reputation.

Acknowledge internally your role as the tangible representative of the unseen God to your children. Ask God's forgiveness and your children's forgiveness for parenting that does not represent a loving heavenly Father. If your parenting is not an accurate likeness, the only righteous course is to own your sin and to show God's true nature through a process of reconciliation.

1 Corinthians 10:13 is your hope and your child's hope. Paul assures you of God's help when you are tempted to sin against your children. This is also a powerful passage to take your children to in their struggle with rebellion.

> No temptation has overtaken you that is not common to man. God is faithful, and he will not let you be tempted beyond your ability, but with the temptation he will also provide the way of escape, that you may be able to endure it. (1 Corinthians 10:13)

What do these words mean? No matter what your temptation is, no matter what your child's temptation is, we can never say, "I just couldn't take any more," or "I couldn't help myself," or "I didn't have any other choice." God will not tempt beyond what his grace provides in Christ. And what is the way out?

Hebrews 4:14–16 describes Christ's high-priestly work in our behalf.

> Since then we have a great high priest who has passed through the heavens, Jesus, the Son of God, let us hold fast our confession. For we do not have a high priest who is unable to sympathize with our weaknesses, but one who in every respect has been tempted as we are, yet without sin. Let us then with confidence draw near to the throne of grace, that we may receive mercy and find grace to help in time of need.
> (Hebrews 4:14–16)

These are amazing words! He sympathizes with our weaknesses. He has been tempted in every way we have, but remained sinless in our behalf. The throne of grace in prayer is open to us as our way out so that we may find mercy and grace to help us when we are tempted. Deliverance is ours when we are tempted.

Christ is our model for parenting, and we are his gospel spokespersons to our children. Here is our parenting hope. We cultivate, plant, and tend. God, through the power of the gospel, brings a harvest!

As we are confronted with a holy God, his righteous law, and our sin, we do not have a God who stands off in the heavens hollering, "Get your act together down there, or else!" We have a loving heavenly Father who, seeing our need, sent his Son to experience life in flesh like ours, to see the world through human eyes, in order that

> . . .he might become a merciful and faithful high priest in the service of God, to make propitiation for the sins of the people. For because he himself has suffered when tempted,

> he is able to help those who are being tempted.
> (Hebrews 2:17,18)

Our children need instruction and discipline that rings true with the call of Christ:

> "Come to me, all who labor and are heavy laden, and I will give you rest. Take my yoke upon you, and learn from me, for I am gentle and lowly in heart, and you will find rest for your souls. For my yoke is easy, and my burden is light."
> (Matthew 11:28–30)

We must understand the resistance in order to make allies of our children rather than adversaries.

Let's review briefly: How might you disarm rebellious children? Begin by understanding their resistance. Think clearly about God's purposes in instructing and disciplining you. Remember that you represent what God is like to your children. This new understanding sets the stage for disarming rebellion!

# 4

# *Spiritual Preparation for Reconciliation*

## *DETERMINE TO MAKE ALLIES OF YOUR CHILDREN*

I was talking to a teenager about the strife in her home. I asked her where she goes to de-escalate when she and her parents are at war. She said, "The bathroom. I am sometimes in there for hours!" I thought that was a strange place to seek refuge until she explained that it was the only place in the house with a lock on the door. The kitchen, living room, hallways, and even her bedroom were the regular battlefields where words and body language were the weapons in ongoing accusations and threats that left all adversaries wounded and weary daily.

Disarming rebellion is our goal. You must have an internal commitment to understanding your child's resistance. Learn to think clearly about God's purposes for instruction and discipline of you. Remember that you represent God before your children. That is your starting place. Change takes place first in you. Then you may begin the necessary preparation for reconciliation. Making allies of your children is not a trick or a strategy, or even your primary agenda. Making allies of your children requires the same internal spiritual commitment as the renewed mind we have already considered.

When parents are at war with teens, an adversarial relationship has taken the place of a meaningful relationship. It is very unusual for teenagers to be in a period of rebellion when there has not been a broken relationship with the parent. You know that's true of adult relationships, too. Whom do you have trouble with in your relationships? It's where something has happened to break the bond in the relationship. That's true in parent-child relationships, too.

So, after understanding the resistance, the next step in the disarming process is to break the cycle of rebellion, to dissolve the adversarial relationship with your child. This is absolutely necessary if you are to make progress. The parent must initiate this. This process of reconciliation must be a settled conviction for you. You must believe that this is God's purpose for you. I can give you these thoughts and ideas, but if God's Spirit doesn't convict you that these things are true, then all of my words will mean nothing when you are confronted with a rebellious teen or a broken relationship with your adult children.

Reconciliation is a big step. It must not be entered into lightly or insincerely. It will unravel in a downward spiral of bitterness into hatred unless parents have settled in their hearts the basic issues of reconciliation. You must determine to make allies of your children in the place of your adversarial relationship.

## SPIRITUAL PREPARATION

Spiritual preparation is a step in God's process for reconciliation in any relationship—not just with your rebellious child. It brings cleansing to your soul, keeping you from giving even more ammunition to a child who is already well armed against you. You know this is true in any relationship. It is so clear in the admonition in Matthew 5:23, 24, regarding worship. *"So if you are offering your gift at the altar and there remember that your brother has something against you, leave your gift there before the altar and go. First be reconciled to your brother, and then come and offer your gift."*

This is significant on three levels. FIRST, God knows our hearts. If you harbor unresolved bitterness, regret, anxiety, or a sense of injustice in your heart toward others, it will get in the way of your worship. God directs his people to resolve such issues so that worship is untainted and can accomplish its goal—to honor God.

SECOND, worship also serves to draw us near to our Sovereign. *"Draw near to me and I will draw near to you. . "* is the resounding promise of God to his people. Drawing near to God was through sacrifice in the Old Testament. After the death of Jesus on the cross, the sacrifices of God are described for us in Hebrews 10.

> Therefore, brothers, since we have confidence to enter the holy places by the blood of Jesus, by the new and living way that he opened for us through the curtain, that is, through his flesh, and since we have a great priest over the house of God, let us draw near with a true heart in full assurance of faith, with our hearts sprinkled clean from an evil con-

> science and our bodies washed with pure water. Let us hold fast the confession of our hope without wavering, for he who promised is faithful. And let us consider how to stir up one another to love and good works, not neglecting to meet together, as is the habit of some, but encouraging one another, and all the more as you see the Day drawing near.
> (Hebrews 10:19–25)

Notice that the thrust of spurring one another on to love and good deeds and encouraging one another comes on the heels of drawing near to God with a sincere heart that has been cleansed from a guilty conscience and purified bodies through the knowledge of and acceptance of Christ's sacrifice for our sins.

THIRD, worship tainted by unresolved issues with others is a deterrent to true worship, and a stumbling block not only to the worshiper, but to all who are affected by the unresolved interpersonal rancor. This is the implication of the words of Jesus in Matthew 5:24. Reconciliation with our brother or sister in Christ is the necessary foundation for the "one-anothering" ministries of Hebrews 10: 24 and 25.

*Personal assessment and a desire for the good of others*

Spiritual preparation must focus first on our own spiritual walk and growth. Biblical self-assessment and a desire for the good and growth of others is the necessary foundation for Christlike reconciliation. Reconciliation fueled by self-interest will fail for two reasons.

FIRST, when we have broken relationships with others, our self-love prevents us from considering the interest of the other person in the breakdown. We are looking for that person to acknowledge his or her fault as a condition for us to be restored! This is true whether the parent is filled with hurt and pain in the relationship, or has become hardened in the relationship and therefore struggles with anger and bitterness toward the child. When we have vested our hope in our child changing or responding well in order for us to feel better about the relationship or to continue our reconciliation efforts, we will quickly grow discouraged and give up.

SECOND, the other person will quickly discern whether our effort is driven by our self-serving needs or it is genuinely driven by love and care for him or her. Let me illustrate: A heartbroken mother might reach out to her rebellious son wearing her heartbreak on her sleeve, and her tears and exclamations of pain will not move the child—teen or adult—to believe that she is driven by love and care for him. Rather, he will believe his mother is desperate for relief from her own broken heart.

Pleas such as, "You don't know how it hurts me when you. . ." do not soften the resolve of the rebellious child (or of the adult child) to stay his ground. On the other hand, the frustrated, angry father will quickly show his colors as soon as his efforts are thwarted by his child's resistance to his efforts, demonstrating to the child that his agenda is to just get this problem behind him and move on with his life.

Outbursts such as "I've had it with you! I can't take any more of your disrespect!" only builds your child's sense of justification against you. Of course, there is also the combination of these two approaches that goes, "We love you, but we also know that you are mocking us behind our backs to your friends. . . ," which leaves the already-hurting and broken teen torn between assurances of love and very real accusations. In all these instances, the teen or adult child will resist any attempts on the part of parents that smack of the parents getting their way. It will feel to the child like more of whatever has already broken the relationship to begin with.

Reconciliation that is fueled by heartfelt, spiritual zeal for personal growth in grace and a true desire for the spiritual well-being of others is heaven-bent for victory. Understand what I mean! The victory may feel one-sided and slow in coming to you, but think of it this way. Your personal victory in initiating and facilitating reconciliation that is concerned with your child's well-being frees your own heart toward your child and clears the way for you to be on God's errand and not your own errand on the road to reconciliation. This is victory for your own spiritual well-being, even if your child is not moved to repentance.

I recently talked to a parent who testified that his efforts to undertake this process with his adult daughter was met initially with suspicion and unbelief. He traveled to her city to talk with her. It took several days of conversation before she was able to receive what he had to say. He acknowledged the ways he had used authoritarian control to direct her behavior without reference to the gospel. He and his wife had been trying for years to re-establish their relationship with their increasingly rebellious daughter through demanding and tense confrontations, without reference to the issues that had created the broken relationships over the years. They were sincere with their efforts and prayed for success, but to no avail. Their daughter felt like all their efforts were just more of the same treatment she had endured throughout her childhood. However, it was her father's persistent but godly acknowledgment, humility, and desire for her good that tore down the walls. This established the foundation for rebuilding a relationship that is mutual and filled with gospel hope.

Philippians 2 is a great window into this mindset. Broken relationships with children, teens, and adult children leave us struggling with selfish ambition and vain conceit (verse 3). We long, even when we are brokenhearted, to be exonerated from any failure in the relationship. We demand, when we feel wronged and misused, to be vindicated. Rather, as God's children (verses 1, 2), the passage calls us to regard the well-being of others above our own interests (verses 3, 4).

> So if there is any encouragement in Christ, any comfort from love, any participation in the Spirit, any affection and sympathy, complete my joy by being of the same mind, having the same love, being in full accord and of one mind. Do nothing from selfish ambition or conceit, but in humility count others more significant than yourselves. Let each of you look not only to his own interests, but also to the interests of others.
> (Philippians 2:1–4)

Then the passage does something amazing! Paul uses Christ as the supreme case study. He says that we are to have the same agenda Christ had. He made himself nothing for the sake of those he loved.

The Master became the servant for the sake of those he would have a restored relationship with—even at the price of his own life.

> Have this mind among yourselves, which is yours in Christ Jesus, who, though he was in the form of God, did not count equality with God a thing to be grasped, but emptied himself, by taking the form of a servant, being born in the likeness of men. And being found in human form, he humbled himself by becoming obedient to the point of death, even death on a cross. Therefore God has highly exalted him and bestowed on him the name that is above every name, so that at the name of Jesus every knee should bow, in heaven and on earth and under the earth, and every tongue confess that Jesus Christ is Lord, to the glory of God the Father. (Philippians 2:5–11)

We could take the analogy further for the sake of our discussion. 1 Peter 2:20–24 reminds us that when Jesus was confronted with his accusers, *"he did not threaten, but continued entrusting himself to him who judges justly."* Why? So that we could be reconciled with God. The cost of genuine reconciliation for the lost was great. The cost of reconciliation of a rebellious child through the initiation of his or her parent will require a servant's heart.

You are realizing by now that spiritual preparation for reconciliation with your rebellious child (regardless of that child's age) must start with getting a servant's heart. You may be tempted to think that solutions in broken relationships will commence when there is change in others. The opposite is true. Reconciliation must begin in the heart of the initiator! Otherwise, you will come to the same impasse all other methods have borne.

Starting with a servant's heart, how will spiritual preparation for reconciliation proceed? What are the implications of initiating reconciliation with others, first having understood their resistance, and then having asked God to give you a servant's heart? The following matters must be in place before you initiate conversation with your child.

***Don't take rebellion personally***

You might be thinking, "Wait a minute. Earlier you were trying to get me to take responsibility for the broken relationship, at least for my complicity in my child's resistance! Now you say, I should not take it personally!" Let me explain. In reality, all rebellion, at its heart, is rebellion against God. The people and circumstances in our lives become the occasion to justify our rebellion. But it is God's law we are breaking with our rebellion. That is true of everyone. When parents take the rebellion personally, they are getting in the way of the child's real adversary in their rebellion—God. This immediately short-circuits that reconciliation process. When we take our child's rebellion personally, we remove the vertical dimension of rebellion against God from our child's consideration. It is as if we are saying, "I am the final authority here. You have to deal with me!"

Spiritually speaking, our child's real problem is his resistance to God's authority. We have to get out of the way so that the real dilemma can be addressed. Our hurt—our indignation about their disrespect, while real and painful—is not the big issue here. When we personalize rebellion, we make it about *us* rather than about *God*. We get in the way of our real goal—to disarm their rebellion. We must be committed to God's agenda rather than preserving our own feelings to promote reconciliation. Otherwise, we will wind up in the same relational cul-de-sac of stalemate and regret.

A middle-aged pastor and wife were incensed when their daughter used a friend's car and played hooky from high school to visit her boyfriend at a nearby university on the day of his music recital. They screamed and threatened her when she arrived home with these words: "You will ruin our ministry! Don't you care about anyone but yourself? All you ever do is break our hearts! Everyone will know about this in no time!" They accused her: "What hotel were you in with this man? You never bring anything but shame to us!"

Now, was there reason for concern for this teenager? Absolutely. Did this teenager need consequences to underscore the great danger she was in and was headed for with her lies, deceit, and disobedience? Absolutely! But God's law and the gospel were completely absent from this interchange. The parents' only consideration was how their teen was affecting them. And the anger and vigor with which they approached their daughter was all about their name and fame, not God's agenda in their lives or their daughter's life or God's glory.

*Give up previous defenses*
As you consider these things, probably one of your greatest struggles is defensiveness. You feel like I am suggesting that this is all your own fault. You feel like someone has to bring some balance to this discussion! Doesn't this child have any culpability? I understand your sense of indignation. But I would once again ask you to hear me out.

Determine before God to rid yourself of defensiveness. Remember, your attitude, body language, and tone of voice will give away what is in your heart, even if you choose the right words.

The disarming process cannot be an attempt to have your child share responsibility for the breakdown in order to demonstrate his or her guilt! It is not another opportunity to rehearse your child's failures and your disappointment in the choices made. You must be prepared to lay aside old hurts. You can't reconstruct the history of the relationship to establish your good intentions or genuine efforts to do the right thing—even though this may be true. Don't try to balance out your failures with successes. "I've tried so hard. . .", "I didn't do everything wrong! Why do you only remember my failures?", "Your brothers and sisters didn't rebel!", or "You know, 50/50 is the only way this is going to work! You have to 'fess up your failures too!" Such efforts and protestations made by hurting parents reek of salving their own consciences and will fail utterly—and the child's antagonism will be deepened and reinforced!

When parents defend themselves in these ways, the child feels internally, and may even say, "You just don't get it!" The child feels unheard and, as a result, feels the need to keep resisting. In fact, the resistance has been reinforced by serial arguments over the same relationship issues.

***Humility is the heart of reconciliation***
Rather, reconciliation has humility at its heart. Seek to understand how your sins and weaknesses, your limitations and insensitivity, have injured, hurt, caused to stumble, and even contributed to the sinful responses of your child or children. Disarming is most powerful as parents learn how they prepared the soil of their child's heart for resistance.

Consider these possibilities. The controlling parent doesn't consider the strengths, weaknesses, preferences, fears, and desires of the child. This leaves the child feeling overwhelmed and bullied by the parent. The angry dad doesn't consider how his lack of restraint may result in everything from fear to a desire for revenge in his child. The pathetic mom plays on the emotions of her child, leaving the child prone to emotional weaknesses or hardening his heart toward compassion for others. The manipulative dad uses rewards and punishments to motivate his child, sometimes referencing God's law as his standard. This either creates a Pharisee who behaves out of self-interest, or a cynic who learns to play the system. The threatening mom uses fear to motivate, leaving her child a captive to the fear of man and/or the desire for the approval of man.

These are only suggestions, but I encourage you to seek God, as David did in Psalm 139: *"Search me, O God, and know my heart! Try me and know my thoughts! And see if there be any grievous way in me, and lead me in the way everlasting!"* What are the ways you may have inadvertently wielded your parenting style to the detriment of your children?

Think about the implications of all these parental methods on your child's character. Character is formed by learned behaviors in childhood. The motivators in a child's life are foundational; they form the worldview. The worldview of your children, therefore, is the treasure house out of which they respond to the people and circumstances of their life. The methods you use to motivate your children have powerful outcomes. Think about the motivations you have used. Colossians 3:23, 24 identify the only worthy motivation.

> Whatever you do, work heartily, as for the Lord and not for men, knowing that from the Lord you will receive the inheritance as your reward. You are serving the Lord Christ. (Colossians 3:23–24)

Reconciliation requires giving up self-defense and justification. True reconciliation requires humility on the part of the person initiating reconciliation!

Our temptation as parents is to justify our parenting style—citing the seriousness of the issues, the failures of others, the "difficult" child, the necessity of maintaining authority, facing hard times, etc.

Parents of adult children sometimes even blame their child's spouse for their broken relationship. I am not denying that a son-in-law or daughter-in-law can have issues that contribute to broken relationships, but the healthy parent-child relationship will usually weather these struggles. If there are some latent offenses in the child's heart toward the parents, it can be brought to expression by the spouse's experience. But the natural loyalty and familial love in healthy parent-child relationships usually protects against the child siding with his spouse against his parents. Obviously, there may be cases where a spouse's needs and behavior leave a child in the impossible dilemma of choosing between relationships. This is tragic and requires great spiritual wisdom, maturity, and compassion on the part of the parents.

We may be tempted to cite our similar struggles as a child, teen, or young adult to say, "Hey! My parents were rough on me, but I just took it and got over it! Why are kids today such wimps?" Until we give those arguments up and recognize that we, wittingly, or unwittingly, hurt and confused our children and acknowledge that we have represented God in flawed ways, we will not disarm our children in their sense of justification and rebellion against us.

None of this is to say we did *everything* wrong—but acknowledging our failures is much more "disarming" than defending our successes! This is the case in parenting, just as in marriage or work relationships.

***Understand the balance between shaping influences and the Godward orientation of your child's heart***[1]

Shaping influences are all the experiences of children's lives that contribute to the way they think about the people and circumstances of their lives. Family life, marriage, divorce, siblings, deaths of family members, moves, physical disabilities, financial prosperity or poverty, work layoffs, popularity, skills and limitations—all of these and more shape the way children think and respond to life. But shaping influences are not the only factor in our children's worldview and responses. The other factor is the Godward orientation of their hearts. They, like everyone, either worship God and look at the world through redeemed eyes, or they bow before the idols of secular culture. Those idols are self-love and self-indulgence, pride, popularity, wealth and fame, to name just a few.

Some parents are defensive because they fear that their "shaping influences" are the *only reason* for their child's rebellion. Mothers especially blame themselves and think, "If only I had done things differently, my child would not have become rebellious!" These parents believe that their child's rebellion is a direct result of their failures or the life circumstances they could not orchestrate. It is true that circumstances we cannot control intrude on our plans and our children's lives. It is also true that we reap what we sow and that our sins produce a bitter harvest. But rebellion in the child's heart cannot be understood simply as the result of unexpected life circumstances or parental failure. Our children make choices based on their relationship with God, and how they interpret life.

Other parents might try to deny that their shaping influences or the unplanned events of life figure into their child's rebellion in any way. "It doesn't matter what we do or say! He's going to do what he's going to do!" This is just as wrongheaded as the previous misconception. It is because the shaping influences of our homes, even the unexpected, have an impact on our children, that we are considering how to bring about reconciliation.

Our children are always interacting with the shaping influences of life. They are deciding whether to allow their own

1 See Tedd Tripp, *Shepherding a Child's Heart,* Second Edition (Wapwallopen, PA: Shepherd Press, 2005), 9–27.

wisdom and experience to interpret the shaping influences, or to believe God and his revelation in Scripture. This biblical balance between shaping influences and Godward orientation relieves parents of the burden of primary responsibility for their child's rebellion. There is no doubt that parents provide profound shaping influences. But our shaping influences are *not* the reason for the spiritual direction our children choose. Their Godward orientation is.

We are undertaking this disarming process, not to assuage our guilt, or to change our children's hearts, or to be the determining factor in their spiritual pilgrimage, but to remove the hindrances created by our sin. Then, they may pursue for themselves a life of knowing and loving God. Remember that God bears the reputation *we* have given him as his tangible representative through their childhood and teen years. If it is not an accurate "likeness," the only righteous course for us is to acknowledge our sin and endeavor to show God's true nature through a process of reconciliation. His grace is sufficient both to forgive our sins and to reshape our parenting vision and responses.

The same misunderstanding of shaping influences and Godward orientation exists when parents take credit for a child's faith in God. Parents' shaping influences are not the *reason* for a child's love for God. We cannot take credit for our children's Christian faith. In the same way, we should not live with guilt over their rejection of Christian faith. We are responsible, however, for repenting and making things right—for asking forgiveness for our failure to live out the gospel for our children.

Spiritual preparation is really the foundation of reconciliation. Resist taking rebellion personally. Strive to give up personal defenses. Remember that humility is the heart of reconciliation. Understand the balance between shaping influences and the Godward orientation of your child's heart. These are so important, but they are all really dependent on the primary preparation for reconciliation—prayer.

# 5

# *Pray*

George Hutchinson, a former professor at Colombia International University, would often wisely say, "Do not talk to others about that which you have spoken little to God."

Spiritual preparation is heavy on prayer. We have no assurance that our confession of past failure and honest efforts at reconciliation will restore a relationship and produce change in our rebellious child. Prayer is essential.

### *Pray for God's forgiveness*

Prayer for God's forgiveness is our starting place. We have the testimony of David in Psalm 51:10–17 as a pattern for such a prayer. David confessed his sin. He requested cleansing. He prayed for a clean heart, a steadfast spirit, joy in his salvation, and a willing spirit. These were the prerequisite to his words in verse 13: *"Then I will teach transgressors your ways, and sinners will return to you."* When we humbly confess our sins before God, he loosens our tongues and gives us the right to speak. It is significant that David doesn't mention his specific sins in this prayer. He knows that a pure and cleansed heart is a person's deepest need. He understands that behavior will follow the heart.

### *Pray that you will model the humility of Christ*

Christ is our model. Isaiah 53:7 says that Christ was silent in the face of his accusers. Why? He was not even guilty! He was silent so that he could accomplish his goal—our redemption. He humbled himself for our benefit. We must humble ourselves for our children's benefit—so that the obstacles in our relationship with them can be dissolved and their pathway to God unencumbered by our sin. Christ accomplished perfectly what he enables us to do through his work.

When children have hardened their hearts and justify themselves because their parents have been harsh, uncaring, self-serving, indifferent to their needs and desires, sinfully angry, vengeful, controlling, manipulative, two-faced, inaccessible, proud, or hypocritical, there is only one solution. It is that described in James 4:1–10.

> What causes quarrels and what causes fights among you? Is it not this, that your passions are at war within you? You desire and do not have, so you murder. You covet and cannot obtain, so you fight and quarrel. You do not have, because you do not ask. You ask and do not receive, because you ask wrongly, to spend it on your passions. You adulterous people! Do you not know that friendship with the world is enmity with God? Therefore whoever wishes to be a friend of the world makes himself an enemy of God. Or do you suppose it is to no purpose that the Scripture says, "He yearns jealously over the spirit that he has made to dwell in us"? But he gives more grace. Therefore it says, "God opposes the proud but gives grace to the humble." Submit yourselves therefore to God. Resist the devil, and he will flee from you. Draw near to God, and he will draw near to you. Cleanse your hands, you sinners, and purify your hearts, you double-minded. Be wretched and mourn and weep. Let your laughter be turned to mourning and your joy to gloom. Humble yourselves before the Lord, and he will exalt you.
> (James 4:1–10)

James is not writing to unbelievers here. He calls them brothers. But he describes their motives and behavior as identical with those of the unbelieving world. His solution to their spiritual idolatry is not that they should shape up and do better. Likewise, our response should not merely be a determination to change. We are not simply turning over a new leaf. This calls for repentance.

Notice the ten qualities of repentance listed in verses 7 to 10.

—*Submit yourselves, therefore, to God (verse 7).* Submission to God is the logical response to God's opposition to the proud. That's what "therefore" is there for. Since "God opposes the proud" but gives grace to "the humble," believers should submit to him. Submission is not the same as obedience. Instead, as we surrender our will, humility leads to obedience. In one sense, I am urging you to submit, not to my insights about reconciliation, but to God's Word regarding reconciliation. Putting our thoughts under the light and scrutiny of Scripture is the first step in repentance.

—*Resist the devil.* This is the second of ten commands that are the practical means of repentance. Think of the multitude of temptations that crowd your days. It is not only the obvious temptations to lie and cheat, but the heart temptations on a continuum from self-pity to vengeance and rage. You have to identify them in order to resist them! Resisting the devil in your pursuit for reconciliation will mean saying no to the enemy of your soul. He comes to you with excuses you can use to avoid acknowledging your sin in your relationship with your children. He tempts you to think that the sins and failures of others dwarf your own shortcomings. Then you tend to blame people and circumstances rather than taking responsibility yourself. He tempts you to dwell on the hurt and rejection you feel rather than concern and compassion for your troubled child. He can even tempt you to be angry with my words and harden your heart toward God's Word as you read this book.

—*And he will flee from you.* Resisting the devil will require believing God even in the face of tactile reasons not to. The promise here gives assurance that, as powerful as Satan may be, God gives grace to resist the devil's schemes. The devil uses what you can see and touch and feel to cloud your spiritual senses. Your child's tactile rebellion with looks, words, and actions are Satan's weapons against your faith in God's ways and the unseen world of spiritual reality. Remember what happened when Christ was tempted in the desert to believe in the material world rather than his Father's cosmic reality. He said in Matthew 4:10, *"Be gone, Satan! For it is written, 'You shall worship the Lord your God and him only shall you serve.'"* In that moment, Christ secured this promise for his people. He bound the strong man, Satan, and plundered his possessions in the wilderness (Matthew 12:29). You may be assured that he will flee because of Christ's finished work. It is not a possibility; it is a reality.

—*Draw near to God (verse 8).* These are God's people, but they have wandered away from God due to unfaithfulness and its fruit. In the same way, we can wander away for a variety of reasons when we are at odds with our children. Certainly, one way is through listening to the childrearing methods recommended by our secular culture. That always bears bitter fruit. But there is another subtle way we can wander off. When we are discouraged and bewildered, hurt and frustrated, wounded and defensive, God and his promises can feel unsubstantial and unreal. We can find ourselves licking our wounds or planning the next skirmish rather than quieting our hearts and basking our weary souls in the power of his truth. Scores of Bible passages come to mind with the soul-satisfying provision that attends drawing near to God. Psalm 34 is representative of such passages.

> I sought the LORD, and he answered me
> and delivered me from all my fears.
> Those who look to him are radiant,
> and their faces shall never be ashamed.
> This poor man cried, and the LORD heard him
> and saved him out of all his troubles.
> The angel of the LORD encamps
> around those who fear him, and delivers them.
> (Psalm 34:4–7)

—*And he will draw near to you.* The assurance that God will welcome us back from our wandering accompanies the call to draw near to him. As a child of God, you know the experience of this. When a passage of Scripture, or hymn, or prayer, or the enjoyment of corporate worship captures your thoughts and carries you into God's presence, you are overwhelmed with a sense of his Spirit with you. Your joy and peace at that moment, your enthusiasm for the gospel, your love of all things sacred, is satiated. Why? You have drawn near to God, and he has drawn near to you.

—*Cleanse your hands, you sinners.* James bluntly calls these Christians sinners, showing the extent of their involvement in worldly actions and the extent to which their attitudes had been affected by secular values. But James is identifying their need for both internal and external repentance here. He is telling them, in this verse, to make their conduct pure. Handwashing is external. For our discussion, we could say, refrain from responding to your teen or adult child in worldly ways. There should be no angry, accusing words; no snide remarks; no manipulation; no controlling to get your way. You get the idea.

—*And purify your hearts.* Their thoughts and motives have been sullied by their eager quest for pleasure described in vv. 1–5, resulting in sins of heart and hand. James gets it! External handwashing alone does not solve their problem. For one thing, changing externals only lasts for the moment. The instant they are tempted again, they will fall into the same sinful desires. True change—growth in grace—takes place as the affections of the heart are transferred from false gods to the one, true and living God. In parenting, identifying and acknowledging the "passions [that] are at war within you" (verse 1) regarding your children is the only route to real repentance. Sometimes the passions are even plausible desires. You want a family that glorifies God. But you must ask yourself why you want that. If you want that inordinately so that you look good or your dreams are fulfilled, you have set yourself up on the throne of your heart. You cannot then be happy or find comfort if it doesn't work out, because God's glory has not been your greatest desire.

—*You double-minded.* This powerfully describes the attempt of the readers to love God and the pleasures of the world at the same time. As parents, we can see the danger here in using secular culture's ways with our children rather than submitting to God's clear teaching about everything from instruction and discipline to nurture and motivation. I have been saddened when talking to parents who have given short shrift to "purifying their own hearts" and want to get on to the "handwashing." That's what unbelievers do. There are scores of books that tell you ten easy steps to anything you set your sights on. So these parents say to me, "Just tell us how to have this conversation. We're ready." I know they are not ready because they have never acknowledged their part in the breakdown. If they have, it has been a token acknowledgment only. I know that this will end in disaster.

*—Be wretched and mourn and weep (verse 9).* James uses a progression here that we often miss in our fast-paced, drive-by view of repentance. James works from the inside out.

*Grieving* means to be miserable, to be wretched. He is describing that heartfelt sorrow before God for our spiritual adultery. Have we wept before the Lord for the flawed ways we have represented him to our children? Have we sought his forgiveness?

*Mourning* is passionate grief that cannot be hidden. Have we acknowledged to our spouse and our children God's conviction and his Spirit's work in showing us our sin and our need to be transformed by his work in us? Have we humbly asked their forgiveness?

*Weeping* is outward grief that is visible to everyone. Have we been open and honest with others about our sin and failure and God's convicting and restoring grace in our parenting? I have found that some of my greatest breakthroughs as a counselor of parents is when I have shared with them my struggle with sin—not to commiserate, but to show them the power of God to overcome my weaknesses for his glory and for my children's good.

*—Let your laughter be turned to mourning and your joy to gloom.* When these people pursued the world and pleasure, their lives were filled with laughter and joy. Mourning and gloom are not the state of the Christian, but they must be the response to the sin of spiritual adultery. God never purposes for his children to stay in the "slough of despond." Rather, identifying and acknowledging sin is their pathway to repentance and forgiveness.

As parents, we often want to move from acknowledging our failure and even asking for forgiveness as quickly as possible and with as little humility as possible. This short-circuits our growth and gospel change and sends a negative signal to others that nothing has really changed. Mourning is where the work is done. Psalm 51 is so telling: David is mourning in verses 1–9; he asks God for a pure heart and a renewed spirit in verses 10–12; and verses 13–17 show the fruit of mourning. David has the right to speak to others because he has humbled himself and done the hard work necessary before God.

I love the connection Matthew makes in the Beatitudes

between mourning and comfort (see Matthew 5:4). There are few sorrows that can hold a candle to the grief parents feel over broken relationships with their children. Comfort is elusive when your world is crashing down around you. Mourning before the Lord yields comfort because God is your refuge, an ever-present help in times of trouble.

—*Humble yourselves before the Lord (verse 10).* This humbling is for the sake of repentance for the sin of transferring your affections from God to the pleasures of this world. Acknowledge that God has given you in his Word all that is needed to establish and maintain a healthy relationship with your children. Depend on his Word and the power of his Spirit to guide you through the process of reconciliation when you fear for yourself and your child.

—*And he will exalt you.* God restores those who humble themselves. Lifting us up as parents puts us back in our rightful place as God's agents in the lives of our teens and in a relationship of mutuality with adult children.

***Make confession as may be appropriate***

If we are to disarm rebellion, we must *confess* the ways we have had alliances with the world in our child-rearing methods—even if it was because of ignorance. We must ask *forgiveness* of God and our offended children. We must *humble* ourselves in the repentance process and draw near to God in his Word by his Spirit. In doing so—we disarm our children, teens, and even our adult children. If they resist further, they have nowhere to hide from the conviction of God's Spirit, because we have removed all the justification they felt as a result of our own sin and failures. They must deal with God! We do not want to be an impediment to our children facing the reality of their rebellion against God. Removing our offenses clears the path to God's convicting power.

There is something in the humility of confessing our sins that loosens our tongues and gives us the right to speak. Our children become armed against our ungodly methods of constraining and controlling their behavior. Genuine confession of our parenting failures breaks through the sense of justification our children feel toward us. In time, as children realize that parents really are striving to understand their part in the relationship breakdown, teens (and adults) begin to put down their weapons. Only taking away their armament will open the way for renewed relationship.

We see the same juxtaposition of humility and the right to speak in Philippians 2. What was Christ's motivation in Philippians 2:1–4? He made himself nothing because he had a purpose—our reconciliation! The "therefore. . ." of verse 12 is contingent on imitating Christ's humility in verses 1–11. The result of this posture is that we may "*. . . shine . . like stars in the sky as [we] hold firmly to the word of life. . . .*" (Philippians 2:15–16, NIV)

***Pray for (and with) your spouse***

There is always a great danger for parents to respond in one of two ways in conversation with rebellious children. Either spouses disagree with each other and one spouse takes up the child's offense against the other, or spouses come to each other's defense and feed off of each other's hurts and indignation against their child. Both of these dangers will keep you from disarming your child's rebellion and will give your child additional ammunition. Where there are two parents involved, they must agree on everything they will and will not say, and pray heartily for each other continually. In preparation for when parents are in conversation with their child, they must agree on a way of signaling to each other that it is time to be quiet, or to end the conversation.

I know that there are occasions where spouses cannot be drawn into these issues because they are either not concerned with family life or are unbelievers. I would encourage the believer, where possible, to appeal to the unconcerned or unbelieving spouse for the sake of their children in these areas.

Appeal is a biblical and effective means of bringing needed change to unjust circumstances. Remember Daniel who appealed to the king's steward to allow an alternate diet for him and the king's other trainees to demonstrate the wisdom of following God's law rather than man's law. Appeal must be carried out with courage, confidence in God, and respect for authority.

*Pray for your child*

Parents who are suffering pain and grief in their relationship with a rebellious child tend to interpret things through the lens of their pain and grief. This is understandable because we are emotional beings, but it is not helpful for healing the relationship and does not facilitate godly prayer. Prayer should not become a digest of our desire for our child's change, and the ways that we are hurt and grieved. When that happens, prayer becomes more about us than the lost and needy child. Certainly, prayer for our own or our spouse's agony over rebellious children is appropriate as we struggle with these emotions, but even in those appropriate personal seasons of prayer, God's comfort and provision of Christ for our loss must be our focus.

Pray that you will be freed from your preoccupation with your own devastation so that you can see clearly to pray for specific needs in your child. Think about the misery, lostness, guilt, and loneliness behind your child's growling and disrespect. As you pray for the hold of sin to be broken in your child's heart, pray that this weary, heavy-laden sinner will find rest for his hurting soul. Pray that God's Spirit will bless your efforts to disarm your child's sense of justification for their thoughts or feelings against you as you do the work of listening and asking for forgiveness. Pray that God will do that awakening work that only he can do by his Spirit, to authenticate the truth of the gospel to your child's heart. Pray that you will have the endurance and confidence in God to see this process through, regardless of how long you must endure.

*Pray that you will have the heart of a peacemaker*

Peacemaking actively builds opportunities to restore relationships, even in the face of being misused and misunderstood. The peacemaker initiates loving extension of himself in a relationship, even in the face of possible rejection. The peacemaker is willing to wade through false accusations and inaccuracies in retelling of past events without defending himself. He resists the temptation to make assessments of the relationship or the child. He resists the temptation to bring to light resolutions and remedies for the conflict prematurely. This work reflects an understanding of the contrast between the wisdom from above and the wisdom of the world. Notice that both earthly wisdom and wisdom from above have profound implications for relationships!

> Who is wise and understanding among you? By his good conduct let him show his works in the meekness of wisdom. But if you have bitter jealousy and selfish ambition in your hearts, do not boast and be false to the truth. This is not the wisdom that comes down from above, but is earthly, unspiritual, demonic. For where jealousy and selfish ambition exist, there will be disorder and every vile practice. But the wisdom from above is first pure, then peaceable, gentle, open to reason, full of mercy and good fruits, impartial and sincere. And a harvest of righteousness is sown in peace by those who make peace.
> (James 3:13–18)

Bitter jealousy is that relentless and grievous discontent toward others. Selfish ambition is that insatiable desire for personal advantage. Both of these motivations bring disorder and every vile practice. These are relationship destroyers.

The qualities described in verse 17—pure, peaceable, gentle, open to reason, full of mercy and good fruits, impartial and sincere—are motivated by a desire for the good of others. They are also relationship builders.

This passage is all about relationships. When I counsel parents, I often ask them to illustrate confrontation with their child to understand what brand of wisdom they are reflecting. The lights come on as they recognize that much of their confrontation reflects earthly wisdom. Get specific; be sure to use Scripture to identify prayer points for yourselves.

***Pray that you will have a will to listen***

This won't be easy. All the pride and fears that brought about your failures in the past will rear their ugly heads as soon as your child spills out his hurts and grievances resulting from your failures. The wisdom of the Proverbs helps us to understand the necessity of listening. Listening is the finest art of communication.

A fool takes no pleasure in understanding,
but only in expressing his opinion.
(Proverbs 18:2)

How often are we fools in conversation with one another. Apart from the marriage relationship, there is probably no relationship where this is more prevalent than in parent-child relationships!

The purpose in a man's heart is like deep water,
but a man of understanding will draw it out.
(Proverbs 20:5)

I hear that teenagers clam up when confronted with parental authority and censure. That doesn't surprise me. But I have been amazed at teenagers' ability to identify and describe the concerns of their hearts when confronted with sincere, listening authorities.

I was counseling a teenage girl as Tedd was counseling her parents because the relationship was so broken that life at home had become dangerous for everyone. Everyone was either screaming or silent. All meaningful conversation had ceased. I asked this girl questions based on her worries and concerns for herself and her parents. She felt like I heard her. She would write pages of answers for homework before our next session. She had deep wells of feelings to express. She only needed someone who would listen and take her seriously.

There is one whose rash words are like sword thrusts,
but the tongue of the wise brings healing.
(Proverbs 12:18)

This Proverb speaks for itself. Words have power to either destroy or heal. Pray that you will exercise wisdom and care in choosing your words.

***Pray that you will not give way to fear***
Fear is powerful! Fear can make us do what we don't want to do and keep us from doing what is best. Already-exhausted hearts cringe at the thought of trying another approach with increasingly hostile children. Fear of worsening relationships or even more devastating confrontations can scare parents. Fear can threaten your resolve to plunge into this disarming process. But God's promises are good prayer requests.

Pray for fearlessness based on the reality of 1 John 4:18.

> There is no fear in love, but perfect love casts out fear. For fear has to do with punishment, and whoever fears has not been perfected in love.
> (1 John 4:18)

Pray for the confidence given in Psalm 46.

> God is our refuge and strength,
> a very present help in trouble.
> Therefore we will not fear though the earth gives way,
> though the mountains be moved into the heart of the sea,
> though its waters roar and foam,
> though the mountains tremble at its swelling. . .
> The LORD of hosts is with us;
> the God of Jacob is our fortress.
> (Psalm 46:1–3, 7)

Pray for strength to display God's power and beauty to your struggling, rebellious children. Pray for the presence of the Spirit with you in this effort in 2 Timothy 1:7: ". . .*for God gave us a spirit not of fear but of power and love and self-control.*"

Prayer and God's Word are the only legitimate foundation for us to bring communication to others. We can fall off the horse on either side here. Some parents say, "I have failed so much. How can I ever have the right to speak to my children about their sin?" The reality is that none of us has the right to speak because of our performance. We have the right to speak only because God has spoken. His revelation is always true and sufficient. Other parents may forge ahead without reference to the principles and absolutes of God's Word. The Scripture says of them, *"When words are many, transgression is not lacking, but whoever restrains his lips is prudent"* (Proverbs 10:19).

Jesus proclaims, *"A new commandment I give to you, that you love one another: just as I have loved you, you also are to love one another"* (John 13:34). The last issue for prayer is of the greatest importance for our reconciliation with our children. Pray that you will love as you have been loved.

# 6

# *Pray That You Will Love as You Have Been Loved*

I was counseling parents who learned that their adult child was complicit in mocking them and their church with some of his friends. Of course, they felt the disloyalty poignantly. Their hearts ached. What could they do? They decided to pray. They prayed that God would help them to lay aside the hurt and respond to their adult child and his friends with love and kindness, remembering Christ's response to his abusers in Isaiah 53.

> He was oppressed, and he was afflicted,
> yet he opened not his mouth;
> like a lamb that is led to the slaughter,
> and like a sheep that before its shearers is silent,
> so he opened not his mouth.
> (Isaiah 53:7–9)

Their child never acknowledged the disloyalty, but the parents replaced the hurt and attending tension in their relationship with their child with genuine gospel courage and loving ministry. As a result, they were rescued from deepening anguish of soul themselves and delivered to represent Christ's love to their child and his friends.

1 John 4:9–10 sets the stage for this self-sacrificing love.

> In this the love of God was made manifest among us, that God sent his only Son into the world, so that we might live through him. In this is love, not that we have loved God but that he loved us and sent his Son to be the propitiation for our sins.
> (1 John 4:9–10)

The key to understanding God's love is verse 10, ". . .not that we have loved God, but that he loved us. . . ." God initiates love to us. His love is not dependent on our obedience or love for him. It is not predicated on our reciprocal love. Love is unilateral. Romans 5:8 echoes the thought that God shows his love for us in that while we were still sinners, Christ died for us. God receives us as we are, even in our sin. Love is not a 50/50 arrangement. His love cannot be lost. God's love is not sappy sympathy, indulgent empathy, grandfatherly tolerance, or unrestrained acceptance.

Think of the qualities of God's love for us in comparison to what our culture calls love. Human sympathy means to take part in another's feelings, to commiserate, mostly by feeling sorrowful about his misfortune. Contrary to a weak and sentimental human sympathy, God loved and forgave us when he could have condemned us.

Human empathy involves understanding other people's feelings as if we were experiencing them ourselves. Contrary to an indulgent human empathy, God doesn't simply understand us; he bore our shame and guilt. He made it his own in his prayer in the Garden of Gethsemane, on the cross, and in the grave. I am reminded of a parable, *Ragman* by Walter Wangerin, Jr., where Jesus takes on the agonies of those he meets in life's struggles, and they are transformed while he bears their infirmities.

God doesn't merely tolerate us as if he were a doting grandparent. He lavishes us with mercy. But his acceptance of us is not detached or permissive. He forgives us for the purpose of transforming us into the likeness of his Son. His acceptance is unrestrained because of his unmerited grace. But his objective in forgiving us (even before we have acknowledged our sin) is our redemption. He perseveres by leading us into truth for the sake of our transformation. That is what God's love is like!

To understand God's love, we must look at his love for his children as our model for loving others. I believe this is where we struggle with loving others, especially our family members. It is easy to feel torn between the call to love as God loves, and the fear of tolerating or overlooking the behavior of others in the name of love. So Christians waver between efforts at acting in a loving way and frustration with remaining silent about the ungodly behavior of others. Parents ask, "Won't my rebellious teen or wayward adult child interpret 'unconditional love' as my approval of his ungodly behavior or worldly appearance?" "Others will think this is all okay with me if I allow my teen to ——, it will look like I accept this." We can answer these questions by looking at the connection between God's love for us and his call to love others in the same way.

What is the connection between God's love and our love? Again, the words of 1 John 4 hold the answer. This is our model.

> Beloved, let us love one another, for love is from God, and whoever loves has been born of God and knows God.
> Beloved, if God so loved us, we also ought to love one another.
> We love because he first loved us.
> (1 John 4: 7, 11, 19)

Since God is the author and source of love, and we are his offspring, it is natural that our love will imitate God's love. Children imitate their parents. You know this is true. The adage "The apple never falls far from the tree" is our experience in life. We sometimes even protest against our upbringing when we say, "I will never do that to my kid when I'm a parent." Guess what? That is exactly what we are tempted to do!

Think about this. We give God a reputation. Our children cannot see this God that we have placed before them since their earliest memory. They know him first through the way we represent him. Our children learn what he is like from what we are like. If we are harsh, self-serving, and distancing, they will believe that is what this Heavenly Father is like. If we are loving, self-sacrificing, and accessible, that is what they will think this Heavenly Father is like.

There is both a promise and a warning in this passage from 1 John. Glimpses of the promise are in verses 12–16.

> No one has ever seen God; if we love one another, God abides in us and his love is perfected in us.
>
> By this we know that we abide in him and he in us, because he has given us of his Spirit. And we have seen and testify that the Father has sent his Son to be the Savior of the world. Whoever confesses that Jesus is the Son of God, God abides in him, and he in God. So we have come to know and to believe the love that God has for us. God is love, and whoever abides in love abides in God, and God abides in him.
> (1 John 4:12–16)

We are able to love as we are loved because *"God abides in us and his love is perfected in us," "we abide in him and he in us . . . he has given us of his Spirit."* God lives in us and we live in God. We know and rely on the love God has for us.

Here is gospel-powered enablement! We don't have to crank up Adam's will to pull off this amazing selfless love. It is resident in us because we are royalty, owned and accepted by God because of our Elder Brother, Christ. Look at Jesus' prayer in John 17:6–19. He makes wonderful references to the supernatural transaction that commissions us because of his completed work. He lived perfectly because we could not. He died as a worthy sacrifice for our sins. He was raised as a witness to God's acceptance of his work, and he now intercedes for his own. All that we need to love our children in the troubled waters of our relationship is ours in Christ. We don't access it by self-effort or a stiff upper lip. We access it through prayer that our love for our children will be attended by God's Spirit at work in us to love them as he has loved us.

We have this sober warning in 1 John 4.

> Anyone who does not love does not know God, because God is love. . . .
>
> By this is love perfected with us, so that we may have confidence for the day of judgment, because as he is so also are we in this world. There is no fear in love, but perfect love casts out fear. For fear has to do with punishment, and whoever fears has not been perfected in love. We love because he first loved us. If anyone says, "I love God," and hates his brother, he is a liar; for he who does not love his brother whom he has seen cannot love God whom he has not seen. And this commandment we have from him: whoever loves God must also love his brother.
> (1 John 4:8; 17–21)

There are two considerations regarding our love for others in this passage. First, John recognizes that the opposite of love is not indifference. It is hate. God calls us to love others so that they will see in us his glory, his attitudes, and his love. We will not do it perfectly, but even in our imperfections, as we strive by his Spirit to genuinely love, he will cause us "to shine like stars in the universe as we hold out the words of life" (see Philippians 2:15). Indifference and disinterest do not proclaim his glory, attributes, and love. In fact, they reek of self-interest. They feel like hate to others. We cannot be neutral.

Secondly, we can love others with confidence because, through Christ's work, we are accepted by the Father. We are free from the fear of man and we are assured of God's love and acceptance through Christ's sacrifice.

When Christ dined with the publicans and sinners, the Pharisees were delighted and the disciples were distressed. But Jesus was not concerned that the publicans and sinners might misinterpret his interest in them as disregard for their sin. He was not worried about how the Pharisees or his own disciples would regard his involvement with the publicans and sinners. He had a motive—love. He had an agenda—the gospel. His goal was not permissive acceptance of their sin. It was to enter their world so that he could bring them the life-giving truth they needed to hear for their salvation.

We must realign our perspective. The challenges parents face with their children in the twenty-first century are not easy. We live in times when gender, marriage, and moral and ethical standards are under attack. Everything that has defined Western culture is disintegrating. There is nothing sacred about Western culture; it has failed at many points. But the historic, biblical foundation of Christian thought that shaped Western culture is consistent with God's agenda—his glory and man's ability to flourish in his creation. Should the Christian mother attend her child's same-sex wedding? Should Christian parents accept and embrace a grandchild born outside marriage? Should Christian parents welcome a child and unmarried partner to their home for family gatherings? Christ would answer with passages such as Matthew 9:9–12, Mark 2:17, and Luke 5:32. A summary of these passages might be, "Yes, I did not come to save the healthy, but the sick. My love for the lost is displayed in my presence with them. I will bring them the gospel."

As for the publicans and sinners, they knew who Jesus was. They knew his message. They weren't thinking, "Look, now, he is one of us. We have changed his mind." But he drew them into his confidence by accepting their invitation to dine with them. He entered their world for the sake of their redemption. He did the same for people like you and me. He didn't stand off in heaven reproving us for our bad behavior. He came into our world, robed in flesh like yours and mine. He looked at the world through our eyes. Why? Hebrews 2:5–18 and Hebrews 4:14–16 warm us with a sense of his love. He was *"made like his brothers in every respect, so that he might become a merciful and faithful high priest in the service of God"* (Hebrews 2:17). He is not *"unable to sympathize with our weaknesses, but one who in every respect has been tempted as we are, yet without sin"* (Hebrews 4:15). We have a high priest who is able to sympathize with our weaknesses because he was tempted in every way—just as we are. That's love! Think of it this way. Love doesn't obscure the law; love precedes the law. If the law preceded love, we could live very successfully and handily by legalism. Of course, the Pharisees demonstrated how well that works! There's an old hymn that goes,

*O Love that will not let me go,*
*I rest my weary soul in thee;*
*I give thee back the life I owe,*
*That in thine ocean depths its flow*
*May richer, fuller be.*

*O light that followest all my way,*
*I yield my flickering torch to thee;*
*My heart restores its borrowed ray,*
*That in thy sunshine's blaze its day*
*May brighter, fairer be.*

*O Joy that seekest me through pain,*
*I cannot close my heart to thee;*
*I trace the rainbow through the rain,*
*And feel the promise is not vain,*
*That morn shall tearless be.*

*O Cross that liftest up my head,*
*I dare not ask to fly from thee;*
*I lay in dust life's glory dead,*
*And from the ground there blossoms red*
*Life that shall endless be.*[2]

Notice that God's Word says in scores of passages, "He who loves me keeps my commands." We don't keep the Law to procure God's love. His love draws us to him so that our love for him causes us to long to obey his law.

The same is true of parental love. Our laws, our authority, our nurture and discipline will not be secured through our insistence. Proverbs 20:28 reminds us that the king's throne is made secure by love. Like Christ, we want to enter our children's world with the motive to love them as we have been loved and with the agenda to bring them the life-giving message of the gospel.

We could marshal scores of passages that remind us that our love is to mirror God's love. 1 Corinthians 13 is a powerful reminder of God's call to love. Think of the qualities of love chronicled there. It highlights the enduring nature of love and denies any self-indulgent or unprincipled motivation toward dealing with others. Consider each of these in reference to your teen or adult child.

> Love is patient and kind; love does not envy or boast; it is not arrogant or rude. It does not insist on its own way; it is not irritable or resentful; it does not rejoice at wrongdoing, but rejoices with the truth. Love bears all things, believes all things, hopes all things, endures all things.
>
> Love never ends. As for prophecies, they will pass away; as for tongues, they will cease; as for knowledge, it will pass away. (1 Corinthians 13:4–8)

We would benefit from pausing at each of these familiar qualities to consider their impact on our daily encounters. What follows is just suggestive of scores of applications of these love qualities.

2 George Matheson, *O Love that will not let me go*

- Patience when we're ready to go and others are procrastinating over tasks that should have been done earlier.
- Kindness when others fail and we have been inconvenienced.
- Joy for others rather than envy when others are praised and we feel overlooked and unappreciated.
- Allowing the lips of others to praise us and not our own lips.
- Taking the smaller role in an event when we feel we would have been better suited for the bigger role.
- Keeping the failures of others to ourselves rather than using their misfortune to promote ourselves.
- Allowing others to choose the biggest piece of pie or to be first at bat rather than seeking the advantage for myself.
- Restraining our anger by thinking the best of the motives and behavior of others, rather than the worst.
- Not reminding others of past hurts to provide our justification for our current offenses toward them.
- Holding back our opinions and commentary on people and circumstances until we have all the information necessary to be gracious and equitable in our judgments.
- Resolving not to be critical of others.
- Having wisdom to discern what is best, and to trust God for our well-being even when we are not sure of others' motives.
- Remembering that God can bring about change where it seems impossible for change to take place.
- Having endurance and keeping our eyes on the unseen world even when all looks hopeless in the seen world.
- Knowing that when we love, we are not trying to achieve our desires as a prize for loving; we are simply responding to a loving Heavenly Father who teaches us this through his Word:

  Dear friends, let us love one another, for love comes from God. Everyone who loves has been born of God and knows God. Dear friends, since God so loved us, we also ought to love one another.
  (1 John 4:7)

Love never fails. I don't believe that Paul is saying that we will never fail in our efforts to love as God loves. Rather, Paul is contrasting the unfailing quality of Godlike love to the fallible and transitory qualities of man's endeavors. In verses 8–12, Paul is comparing the seen with the unseen, the temporal with the eternal, and the finite with the infinite. He is saying, "You can bank on God."

> As for prophecies, they will pass away; as for tongues, they will cease; as for knowledge, it will pass away. For we know in part and we prophesy in part, but when the perfect comes, the partial will pass away. When I was a child, I spoke like a child, I thought like a child, I reasoned like a child. When I became a man, I gave up childish ways. For now we see in a mirror dimly, but then face to face. Now I know in part; then I shall know fully, even as I have been fully known.
> (1 Corinthians 13:8b–12)

Do our words, attitudes, responses, and body language toward our children, regardless of their age, mirror these love qualities? There are no caveats here about who is worthy of such love. This love is universal. Notice Paul's assessment in verses 1–3.

> If I speak in the tongues of men and of angels, but have not love, I am a noisy gong or a clanging cymbal. And if I have prophetic powers, and understand all mysteries and all knowledge, and if I have all faith, so as to remove mountains, but have not love, I am nothing. If I give away all I have, and if I deliver up my body to be burned, but have not love, I gain nothing.
> (1 Corinthians 13:1–3)

It is significant that many religious practices and fondly held traditions are not of the greatest value in God's economy. Tongues, prophecy, and even faith and benevolence pale in comparison to love. In fact, the most lofty spiritual callings of faith and hope are subservient to love. *"So now faith, hope, and love abide, these three; but the greatest of these is love."*

I don't know why Paul ends the love chapter with this statement. But we could conjecture that our sinful natures would turn faith and hope to serve our own desires without the qualities of love that God demonstrated in giving what was most precious to him, his own Son, to achieve our redemption.

Understanding the spiritual dimensions of preparation is a necessary first step to disarming your rebellious child. You will experience relationship meltdown if you initiate conversation and are not convinced in your own heart of the wisdom of God's way to reconciliation. Prayer to love as God loves is paramount.

In all these efforts, we must exhibit the fruit of the Spirit (Galatians 5:22–23) and make use of the whole armor of God (Ephesians 6:10–20). Remember, this is not another exercise in behaviorism. This is a spiritual endeavor—a holy mission. Be sure your own heart has known the Master's plow—that strong roots and good fruit are evident. Otherwise, your work will be in vain and you will reap harder hearts than before! Our hope is this: *"And a harvest of righteousness is sown in peace by those who make peace"* (James 3:18).

If you are thinking now, "You just don't know my teenager!" you're right. I don't. But God does. And he is able to make your humble obedience to his truth effective and productive in your home!

# 7

# *Practical Preparation for Reconciliation*

I asked a father about how he thought he and his wife were doing with their spiritual and practical preparation for reconciliation. He said, with all sincerity, "We're planning on talking to John on Thursday. We will have a couple hours that morning to get through all that." After picking my chin up off the floor, I chided him, "That is like patching a rusted gas tank with Bondo! Either you'll lose all your fuel, or a spark will send you up in smoke!" Spiritual and practical preparations for reconciliation are critical and worthy of your time.

Prayer will be the fruit of spiritual preparation and the essential foundation for practical preparation for reconciliation. You are reading this because an adversarial relationship has filled the void of meaningful relationship with your child, whether he is twelve, twenty, or thirty-five. Your agenda is reconciliation. You must initiate the process, first through spiritual preparation, then by considering the necessary practical needs that lie ahead. Don't think, "Well. okay, I'll give it a try, but if the kid doesn't respond—I'll give up!" You're embarking on a process of healing. You may have some difficult hurdles. If your child sees and hears godly resolve in your voice and attitude, it will help the process. If he gets a sense that you're making one last effort and he "had better get it right," you're sunk before you begin!

Reconciliation cannot be to feel better, to get it off your chest, to get on with life, to justify yourself, or to clear your conscience. It must be about the spiritual well-being of your child and the praise of God.

How can you approach your child? It might sound like this. "I've been thinking about our relationship. I know our struggles with each other must be as difficult for you as for me. Let's give some thought to when we can talk. I know it will take time, understanding, and patience with each other, but I sincerely want to have reconciliation. I will really try to go at a pace you feel comfortable with. Will you think about it and get back to me?"

This is so important. You must have this determination to endure what will surely come. Humble yourself to hear both accurate and inaccurate accounts of your parenting. You may even hear from your daughter-in-law or son-in-law things that have been reported about your parenting that will break your heart. You must remember, "This is my son." "This is my daughter." "I love my child too much to allow this estrangement to continue. I will entrust myself to God and do the difficult work of reconciliation even if it is one-sided. I will mirror the agenda of Christ in Philippians 2:7, how '. . .*he made himself nothing by taking the very nature of a servant. . .*' (NIV)." Why did he do this and what should that demonstrate to us? God the Father and Christ the Son were on a mission of reconciliation! "The Son of Man came to seek and to save the lost." (Luke 19:10). Here are some practical considerations.

## *PLAN YOUR CONVERSATION*

You have already done spiritual preparation (Chapters 4–6) that prepares you for this disarming conversation.

***Be aware of the boundaries in your relationship due to the age and living circumstances of your child***

Perhaps you are undertaking reconciliation with an adult child who has his own family, or a child who has already left your home and is in college or living with friends or relatives. Or you may have an adult child who has returned to your home for any number of reasons. The same principles apply. But you must keep in perspective the differences created by whether you are still providing shelter, food, and parental oversight for your child or he is living on his own or as an adult in your home. While the principles are similar, obviously your relationship boundaries are different. This requires wisdom and care.

***How are the boundaries different?***

Your attitude and commitment to the process of reconciliation will be identical, regardless of the age and living arrangements of your child, but your approach will necessarily take these matters into consideration. A child living in your home still has some dependence on your provision of food and shelter, and an obligation to respect the standards and atmosphere created by his presence in your home, whether he is sixteen or twenty-five.

It is important to stop here to nuance the lines between a teen under your responsibility and direction, and an adult living in your home.

For example, leaders in the home have explicit direction in Exodus 20:8–11 regarding the keeping of the Sabbath day. The law extends to everyone in the house—whether son, daughter, manservant, maidservant, animals, and aliens. The privilege and responsibility of leadership of the household regarding God's commands and promises is extended throughout the Old Testament. It is not presumptuous or authoritarian for parents to set the atmosphere for their home. The problem, however, may arise from how that is undertaken. Harsh and unloving application of God's law not only alienates children of all ages; it also disfigures God's purpose in giving the law—to protect and preserve his people. As a parent, you have the privilege and responsibility to have your home reflect God's ways, but you also have the duty to accurately reflect the loving and compassionate authority of your Shepherd. This is always true with your children, but there is special significance in the case of adult children living in your home. You may require that the standards for your home be respected and adhered to even by your adult child, but you must also show your adult child the respect and dignity of his status as an adult.

How do you do that? Your attitude, speech, and demeanor should have the same Christian character qualities you would extend to any adult: love, goodness, kindness, gentleness, understanding, patience, and self-control. Mocking, the silent treatment, dirty looks, gossip to others, withholding of attention or affection, and derogatory or dismissive comments have *no place* in the Christian home in response to children, whether young or old. Such behaviors are absolutely counterproductive to everything you long for. They destroy.

Of course, the boundaries for an adult child living independently are obvious. He has a sense of detachment connected to his ability to make his own choices for standards and atmosphere in his home. You cannot impose your sensibilities on him.

***Suggested conversation starters***

FOR YOUR CHILD living in your home, you might begin in this way after establishing the need for a conversation (see the suggested comments above and suggestions coming later in the chapter).

"I am so thankful for your willingness to talk with us about our lives together. I think our struggles with one another have been as difficult for you as they have been for us. What do you think?" Allow time for your child to respond.

"Let me begin by acknowledging that we know you have felt angry and frustrated with us. Living together creates a lot of opportunities for hurts and frustrations to fester. Have you noticed that?" Allow your child to respond.

FOR YOUR TEEN... "On the one hand, you seem to be growing in your sense of preferences and you are probably internally making choices that are different than the path we are on. Do you feel that way?" Allow your child to respond.

FOR YOUR RESIDENT ADULT... "We know that you have made lifestyle choices that are different than ours. We want to respect your right to make independent choices." Allow your child to respond.

"We have felt the responsibility to create and maintain the atmosphere and standards in our home that are in keeping with our spiritual commitments. I think this is one of the things that has put us at odds with one another. What do you think?" Allow your child to respond.

"We believe that we can understand and sympathize with some of the ways we have contributed to our breakdown. We love you and want to determine, with your help, how we can live together in ways that resolve your frustration with us and that also allow us to continue to maintain the peace of our home. Can you think about beginning this conversation with us?"

FOR YOUR ADULT CHILD who is living independently of you, you might begin in this way after establishing the need for a conversation. Notice that it is important for all these conversations to be dialogue, not a monologue.

"We appreciate your willingness to talk with us about our

relationship. Have you felt like we have been through this many times before and it hasn't helped?" Allow your adult child to make a response.

"Probably, in many ways, your independent life has diffused some of the daily frustration you have felt when you were living at home. But we want to ask you to bear with us. We love you and long to have our relationships healed. Do you feel that you can undertake this with us?" Allow your adult child to make a response.

"We have come to see things in a different light from when you were growing up. We realize that we have contributed to the breakdown in our relationship in ways we have not understood or acknowledged before. We want to be open to hearing and acknowledging both the attitudes and the occasions that have created this alienation between us. I guess we are asking you to participate in that process." It would be good at this point to illustrate one of the ways you have sinned against your child—perhaps with a judgmental spirit, anger, manipulation, or negatively critical spirit. Continue with, "Does that sound familiar to you? We know there must be other ways we have hurt you. We want to talk to you about those things." Allow a response from your adult child.

"We love you and want to be able to participate in your adult life, and you in ours, in ways that respect the different paths we have taken, but allow us to have healing as well." Give some time for a response.

***DON'T RUSH! Schedule a time that is not hurried by your responsibilities or your child's schedule***

Spiritual issues don't respond easily to time pressure or impatience. Don't try to have the conversation recommended here in response to an event of rebellious behavior, a time of correction over specific issues, or a breakdown with adult children. Your teen or adult child will be least responsive when he believes he must defend himself.

Your temptation will be to get this conversation behind you. Where our emotions and our children are involved, we have a sense of urgency that often keeps us from choosing the best way forward. So, be careful and deliberate about choosing the best time to pursue this conversation with your child. Block out sufficient time to prepare yourself for it, but also to facilitate an uninterrupted time.

Have the same consideration for your child. If your child is living at home, his schoolwork, extracurricular activities, and even his free time shouldn't be forfeited unless he is agreeable. Your conversation should not feel like punishment to your child.

If you have an adult child living at home, you must maintain the fine line that respects your responsibility to preserve and maintain the biblical atmosphere you have for your home, but that also respects the fact that you are no longer the authority who makes decisions for your adult child. This requires special care and may necessitate a preliminary conversation with an adult child returning to live with you.

Adult children living with parents are responsible to respect and cooperate with the spirit and standards of the home that is providing shelter for them. It is not a dorm or peer housing arrangement. Consideration for family schedule and duties is appropriate. The fine line here is to work through how to interact with your adult child to navigate differences in lifestyle, moral and ethical considerations, and the stuff of daily life. All the elements we have already considered apply.

If your child is living independently, appeal to him to consider a time in his schedule that would give you time to talk together for a period of time—perhaps an hour, two hours, or whatever would facilitate meaningful conversation. Face-to-face conversation is always preferable, but in this age of social media, there are also many ways of conversing face-to-face over long distances. Facial expression and body language are essential to conversations that will disarm your child, so phone calls are not productive. Misunderstandings and further damage can result from an inability to read each other with more than words exchanged over the phone or via written communication alone.

***Be prepared for the best and for the worst***

There is no way to know what path your conversation with your teen or adult child will take. You must be prepared spiritually and practically for all possibilities.

If the conversation becomes heated, you must be prepared to bring the conversation to a peaceful end and recommend how to proceed another time. You might say, "I sense that we are struggling to have a constructive conversation. Continuing will not accomplish our goal to love and understand each other. Let's pray and ask God to help us consider the things that have been said and prepare our hearts to talk again when we have had time to think these things through." You will be tempted to be discouraged if the conversation doesn't go well, but remember that this is a process. Your response to the conversation and willingness to persevere is really more important than how well the conversation goes. If you end the conversation with grace, you will have another opportunity to make strides toward reconciliation.

If the conversation is going well, the temptation will be to press on and accomplish more than is advisable in one event. Remember that this is for your child, whether he is fifteen or thirty-five. Extending the conversation will tax your child's patience and ability to process what is being said. Don't go beyond your plan for the conversation. Unscripted or unplanned territory can lead to reckless words and emotional meltdowns.

***Have the setting be as relaxed as possible***

If your child is living at home, be sure that younger (and older) siblings will not interfere and that you have privacy to carry on the conversation. Your teen's favorite drink or snack wouldn't hurt, too! I have talked to parents who have tried to have this conversation with their teen is the same place the child associates with previous arguments. This conversation conjures up in the child's mind more of the same. While I believe those "spaces" can be redeemed by new ways of communication, it might not be the best place to start. Choose a neutral place—perhaps the child's room, the patio, or some place that is not closed in or dark.

If your child is living independently, ask your child to identify the best place to meet, perhaps at his home. This gives your child a sense of your desire to participate on his terms rather than demanding your own preference. Where distance prevents an in-person meeting, ask your child what video-chat platform will serve your efforts best.

***Don't spring the conversation on your child***

If your child is living at home, suggest possible times you could talk together. See when he is available. Tell him you want to share some things you've been thinking about regarding your relationship. Tell him you are interested in him responding with his thoughts as well.

If your child is living independently, depending on the distance involved, you may need to be patient for a response to a request to talk together. Work and family responsibilities may necessitate some careful planning to see things through.

***Be sure (where your spouse is involved), that you have discussed the content of this conversation beforehand***

If your child is living at home, there may be benefit to your spouse participating in the conversation, especially if both parents have been complicit in the relationship breakdown and both parents long for reconciliation with their child. As I noted in the last chapter, it is essential that parents have agreed together about the content of the conversation. There should not be any surprises that will undermine your primary goal—to converse with your teen. If you are easily drawn into negative responses with your child, plan and pray for your struggle and for positive, godly responses in the place of former responses. You know many of your child's typical responses to past confrontations, so you can plan together new ways to interact that create a non-threatening atmosphere. Parents must help each other to overcome threatening and accusing or confrontational language and behavior. Otherwise, your child will feel ganged up on. Try to anticipate how your child may respond to you and then plan godly, positive responses to the possible responses made.

## *REMEMBER YOUR SPIRITUAL PREPARATION*

You must be prepared spiritually to lead your child to spiritual considerations. It is as important for you to have your own heart prepared by God's Spirit for the audience you will have with your child as it is for the pastor to have labored in prayer and in the Scriptures over the preparation of his sermon to the congregation. Scores of well-meaning parents have begun an impromptu conversation with their child without spiritual preparation that has ended in disaster. Why? Perhaps the energy behind the encounter was the parents' sense of emotional urgency over some event or pattern in family life that grieved or angered the parent. Generally, when parents use Scripture in this context, it is not for the gospel hope and Christ's sufficiency for the moment, but rather as proof texts to justify the parents' hurt or grievance. If your child is living at home, consider the following:

Don't try to have the conversation recommended here in response to an event of rebellious behavior or at a time of correction over specific issues. You will struggle with the temptation to respond emotionally or defensively out of personal hurt. Your child will be most resistant when he believes he must defend himself. I have talked with scores of teens and young adults who have reported their parents saying things like this. "I love you and I am committed to you *but* I know that you. . .", and the parents go on to accuse, and hurt their child—making a lie of their professed love and commitment. Children, no matter their age, have a keen sense of your intentions, usually borne of scores of previous encounters. Often, their response to your current conversation bears the hurts and memories of the outcome of many previous confrontations.

Work to change this dynamic in your relationship with your child. Make your times of conversation nonconfrontational. Remember that this is about redeeming a relationship more than the crisis of the moment. You are after more than solving the immediate problem. You want your conversation to bear lasting fruit, both in discipleship and in your relationship. Your hope in God, your agenda to disciple your child rather than to simply punish his infractions, and your willingness to share responsibility for the breakdown will create a new atmosphere in which your child will listen. He may not agree, but he will begin to feel that this is something you are doing *for* him, not *to* him.

2 Timothy 2:24–26 both warns and directs productive and restorative conversation.

> And the Lord's servant must not be quarrelsome but kind to everyone, able to teach, patiently enduring evil, correcting his opponents with gentleness. God may perhaps grant them repentance leading to a knowledge of the truth, and they may come to their senses and escape from the snare of the devil, after being captured by him to do his will.
> (2 Timothy 2:24–26)

Notice the qualities of speech here—kindness and gentleness. Avoid attitudes and words that are quarrelsome and resentful. I call these inflammatory words—they invite controversy. Use words that are full of hope. And notice your goal: it is the spiritual good of your opponent. In Paul's instruction to Timothy there is no hint that there should ever be anger, defensiveness, proving one's point, or personal vindication.

If your child is living independently, you will have the same concerns already mentioned. However, your role is different in relationship to adult children. You are no longer in a role of oversight and godly authority in their training. Adult children are independent of your authority. Your adult child must have a sense that you are coming to him in a mutual, peer-level effort to restore the relationship. This doesn't mean that appropriate respect for you as a parent is not warranted. But your child must have a genuine sense that you are in a posture of Christlike humility and that you are coming alongside rather than coming as the authority to bring correction or discipline.

Spiritual preparation, and conversation that is rich with gospel analysis of the struggle with sin, and rich with gospel hope, will be a message your child can receive, even if he or she does not agree with you about spiritual things.

## HOW DOES A PARENT DISARM A CHILD IF A SPOUSE WON'T GO ALONG?

In some circumstances, the child's argument is with one parent and not the other. Often the neutral parent becomes the unspoken mediator between the warring parent and child. This becomes an overwhelming emotional battle for the neutral parent who is being pulled toward both sides and can never appease either.

If your child is living independently, it will be wise to consider what your adult child can deal with. It may be necessary for each parent to talk with the child independently about the parent's new insights and seeing how he, as a parent, has contributed to the broken relationship. It is essential for the parents not to undermine each other in word, expression, or body language. One benefit of both parents being present is that they can help to refine each other's remarks and caution against falling into old patterns of conversation.

***One conversation will not disarm***

It will take ongoing conversations. Don't try to do it all the first time. You will overwhelm your son or daughter and ensure that he or she doesn't want to go through that again! Set limits for yourself with your spouse before you begin so that you don't get "on a roll" and try to get all your thoughts in on the first conversation. Determine to watch and listen for hints from your child that he is feeling overwhelmed or resistant. You know your child well enough to recognize when he cannot go on. Be prepared to allow your child to gauge the length and content of your conversations. Remember that this is a process, not an event.

All the spiritual and practical preparation so far is transforming us in preparation for genuine gospel ministry to our needy child, regardless of his age. That is always the way God works in his children. We are changed so that we can bring the gospel to others. And this holy process will never end until we are confirmed in righteousness at the coming of our Lord Jesus Christ. That's what David is acknowledging in his prayer of repentance in Psalm 51:10–13.

Now, it's time to talk!

# 8

# *It's Time to Talk*

"We need to talk!" is probably not the best way to initiate a conversation with your child. When your child, regardless of his or her age, hears these or similar rehearsed commands, it brings back dramatic scenarios from the past that causes your child to recoil. As I have already noted in earlier chapters, start by acknowledging your new insights and your desire to look at your relationship through new eyes.

Spiritual and practical preparation for disarming rebellion takes time and serious consideration. Do not take the process lightly. It is very difficult to reverse conversations that have gone badly due to insufficient preparation. It won't hurt for you to reread the previous chapters before you start a conversation with your child.

When you're ready, remember that you don't have to accomplish all your goals in your first conversation. Attempting that will probably scare your teen and shut him down. A caution here! Don't add to your planned conversation. If you do, you may end up preaching. Preaching is for pastors in pulpits. Even then, it should always be sweetened with the gospel. Stress that you love him—even if you don't always love his behavior.

Parental talks must always be a dialogue, not a monologue. Ask questions and listen to the answers. They will afford you good insights. All your interactions with your child should reflect love and mercy—even when you are bringing discipline and correction. Don't let these healing conversations turn into another long, exhausting litany of your demands and your child's failures! In fact, be quick to genuinely seek forgiveness when you fall into old patterns in your conversation. If you catch yourself falling into old patterns, you can always say, "I'm doing it again, aren't I? Forgive me. Let's pray and ask God to help me. And then let's start again."

After you have disarmed your teen from his resistance to you, there will be time to graciously and tactfully help him to see his struggle with your parental authority. Then, gently, without accusation or inflammatory language, you may instruct him to a correct understanding of your parenting if his assessment of your parenting is inaccurate. Consider these words of wisdom from Proverbs 16:

The wise of heart is called discerning,
and sweetness of speech increases persuasiveness.
The heart of the wise makes his speech judicious
and adds persuasiveness to his lips.
(Proverbs 16:21, 23)

*New ways of talking*

Begin your conversations by assuring your child of your desire and determination, by God's grace, to learn new ways of interaction that will not foster strife and division between you. Share with him what you are learning about your previous parenting, the role of the gospel in parenting, or your understanding of him.

One such life-altering consideration for you and your child may be that God's agenda is always to make his children holy, not to punish them. Punishment is reserved for final judgment when God will separate the sheep from the goats and usher in eternal punishment for all who have not repented and believed (see Matthew 25:31–46). We certainly will reap what we sow. There are always consequences attached to our obedience to God's ways—blessing. And there are always consequences for our disobedience—destruction. Consequences are designed to remind us of God's purpose to restrain his judgment and to extend his mercy.

Hebrews 12:5–11 is so clear regarding God's agenda in discipline—shown in the word picture of sowing and reaping.

And have you forgotten the exhortation that addresses you as sons?
"My son, do not regard lightly the discipline of the Lord,
nor be weary when reproved by him.
For the Lord disciplines the one he loves,
and chastises every son whom he receives."
It is for discipline that you have to endure. God is treating you as sons. For what son is there whom his father does not discipline?
. . . For the moment all discipline seems painful rather than pleasant, but later it yields the peaceful fruit of righteousness to those who have been trained by it.
(Hebrews 12:5–7; 11)

If you're thinking, "My child isn't a believer," then remember and share the wonderful mercy expressed by Peter:

> But do not overlook this one fact, beloved, that with the Lord one day is as a thousand years, and a thousand years as one day. The Lord is not slow to fulfill his promise as some count slowness, but is patient toward you, not wishing that any should perish, but that all should reach repentance.
> And count the patience of our Lord as salvation. . .
> But grow in the grace and knowledge of our Lord and Savior Jesus Christ. To him be the glory both now and to the day of eternity. Amen.
> (2 Peter 3:8–9; 15, 18)

*Acknowledge sin and failure*
If you think you know of ways that your attitude, speech, or behavior have contributed to your child's resistance to you and the gospel, acknowledge it. Identify your mistakes and why they are wrong. Acknowledge, if appropriate, your mistake in mixing God's direction for parenting with the methods of our secular culture.

*Ask forgiveness for known sins and failures*
Ask for forgiveness for specific failures that you are aware of. Consider these possible areas of failure:

Have you withheld love, affection, and acceptance? Have you been guilty of anger, legalism, manipulation, disapproval (of the emotional sort), shaming, threats, guilt trips, ungracious and inconsiderate responses?

Have you used methods that only change behavior without challenging heart attitudes?

Have you used unfair assessments and accusations, harshness, selfish goals, authoritarianism, and controlling your teen or young adult child rather than being a godly authority?

Repent not just for the wrong response, but also repent for the attitudes of heart that prompted your response. For instance, an angry response is often prompted by pride and a selfish desire to get your way. Unholy anger is never appropriate, even if you believe your cause is right. Righteous anger is focused on maintaining God's law and glory, not getting your way or putting your child "in his place."

*Give your teen an opportunity to respond to your assessment of your failures*

Don't defend past practices; rather facilitate your child's expression of the issues that have made him feel justified in his rebellion. You may have missed something important. Think of it this way: It is possible to defend yourself by appealing to your good intentions and miss the way you have been hurtful.

If you don't know what the specific issues are in your shaky relationship, but you are suspicious that your teen has something against you, tell him that you know there are ways that you have sinned against him and that you want his help to identify them so that they are not in the way of healing your relationship. Encourage him so that you can work together in the future toward a good and godly parent-child relationship. Be quick to genuinely seek his forgiveness when you fall into old patterns.

One of your goals in this conversation is to remove your child's defensiveness. The surest way to accomplish this is to be open and accessible in your own posture and attitude toward your child's assessments—whether accurate or inaccurate—of your parenting. He will begin to learn that defensiveness works against everything you want to promote in relationship.

*Give your child time to "digest" all you have said*

Invite your teen or young adult to respectfully ask questions, to tell you ways your previous methods have hurt and confused him. This may require a period of silence while he thinks how to respond or it might mean setting another time to give your child the needed space to think. You will want to give him help here to respond to your request in ways that are honest and respectful. Your first conversation may not be a time to hear your child's response. It may be better to leave his response until a later conversation. This depends on your assessment of your child and of the situation.

*Help your child by asking questions that will help him verbalize his feelings*

If he is fearful of getting his hurts and resentment out and tends to rebel by withdrawing rather than yelling, you could ask questions like these:

- What are the occasions of your hurt and resentment?
- Do they happen during times of discipline?
- Are there specific things I say or do that trigger these feelings?
- What is it about my interaction with you that causes you to feel like I don't understand you or that you can't even get me to listen?

*Set parameters for his responses*

If your child has no trouble blurting out his resentment and you fear asking him to tell you how you have hurt him, you could speak to him as follows.

"I sincerely want to understand the ways I have contributed to your struggles with our relationship. I believe I have not responded in constructive ways to our arguments in the past. That is why 'talking' has not been productive, but harmful. Let me set these guidelines for your response to my failures. You may tell me the occasions that bring about your sense of hurt and resentment and even the words I use that make you feel angry. You may describe the ways I make you feel and how you interpret my attitude and motives. It will not be helpful or respectful to accuse me or demand responses from me. I will try to help you understand the difference between expressing your feelings and disrespect as we talk. Do you understand?"

Then follow through. Firmly but lovingly direct his interaction with you. It might be helpful to work out some way he can signal to you that he is feeling angry or overwhelmed and that it is time to quit.

*Know when to stop*
In this first conversation, you are really only trying to get the matter out in the open. If that's all you accomplish, it is enough. Your teen will give you hints about his tolerance for going on. If your teen is responding with crying, nervousness, anger, hostility, fidgeting, or seems unresponsive, it's time to take a break. Always be quick to end a conversation that is not going well. End by giving your child hope for the future.

Here are some things to consider about the way you end the first conversation:

*Leave your child with a biblical picture of shepherding*
Tell him that you want to shepherd him in the same way Christ shepherded you—Christ looked at the world through your eyes. Hebrews 2:14–17 is your model:

> Since therefore the children share in flesh and blood, he himself likewise partook of the same things, that through death he might destroy the one who has the power of death, that is, the devil, and deliver all those who through fear of death were subject to lifelong slavery. For surely it is not angels that he helps, but he helps the offspring of Abraham. Therefore he had to be made like his brothers in every respect, so that he might become a merciful and faithful high priest in the service of God, to make propitiation for the sins of the people. (Hebrews 2:14–17)

Verse 17 is remarkable. Christ was made like his brothers in every way *in order to* be a merciful and faithful high priest. Christ came alongside you to comfort and encourage you, even in your sin. He promises to be with you and to help you walk in his ways. Acknowledge to your child that you have not had this perspective and that God has brought conviction to change you—and hope in Christ that you can change. Tell him you want to be like Christ for him.

*Tell your child clearly what you expect of him*
Where specific patterns of rebellion must be addressed while the process of disarming is going forward, tell your child clearly what

you expect of him. Discuss those expectations with him in ways that he can receive. Do everything you can to facilitate communication. Acknowledge that you know how difficult this is for him. Do not present expectations as a new set of rules or hoops to jump through. Rather, present your expectations as standards that you insist on for his good and for God's glory.

For a teen who is still under your care and provision in your home, this might be a scenario: "God has charged us as your parents with your safety and training for responsible adulthood so that you are well prepared for the roles before you in the years to come. Our insistence that you be home at a set time from social activities with friends falls under that concern. This is not arbitrary, and we trust that our standards will prepare you well for the day when you bear responsibility for creating parameters for yourself and those under your care. You will be a better friend to your peers if you have wise and considered parameters when no one is making decisions for you and them."

For the young adult living in your home, this might be a possible scenario: "We are happy that you are living at home through this transition time in your life." (You may want to briefly describe the circumstances that have necessitated their presence in your home.) "As we indicated when you returned home, we want to respect your right to live as an independent adult regarding your schedule and decisions, but we also must retain the atmosphere we believe is appropriate for our home and live together with respect and consideration for one another in the family. While we want to be considerate of your work and your social schedule, we also have asked that you participate in the daily care and maintenance of the home. So the chores we all share to make home pleasant and livable for all of us are essential for family life."

Of course, if you are talking to an adult child living elsewhere, this is not an aspect of your conversation except for the request that, as you talk together, you each respect each other in the attitudes and speech exchanged.

*Tell your child what he may expect from you*

Describe everything from your response to his behavior to the consequences he may bring on himself—that is, sowing and reaping—as a result of his choices. The process we have already covered should lay a foundation that will make your child more receptive of your expectations and consequences. Express encouragement and hope even when you must register concern and alarm for the events and circumstances you are in.

For a teen still under your care and provision in your home, you could continue the scenario from above. "Because our standard for curfew is for your good now and for your future, we insist that you respect and abide by these times. If you are unable to be home on time for a legitimate reason, you must call and talk to us about it before the time arrives. If you continue to arrive home after the set times, we will need to restrict your social opportunities and/or your use of transportation for a time. Our desire in shaping these consequences is not to punish you, but to underscore the important and valuable truth of Galatians 6."

> Do not be deceived: God is not mocked, for whatever one sows, that will he also reap. For the one who sows to his own flesh will from the flesh reap corruption, but the one who sows to the Spirit will from the Spirit reap eternal life. (Galatians 6:7–8)

"You cannot live with success and stability if you ignore wisdom. We want to encourage you to practice restraint that is marked by adherence to mature direction for your life and habits."

For the young adult living in your home, this might be a possible scenario. "We talked about all this when you returned home, and you felt then that these were reasonable and fair expectations. We are happy to discuss any ways you feel that we have not regarded your rights fairly or ways that your thinking has changed. However, even if we need to make adjustments, we must insist that you respect the appropriate expectations that our home reflect an atmosphere and cooperation in accordance with our values and beliefs."

Of course, again, if you are talking to an adult child living elsewhere, this will not be an aspect of your conversation.

***Close the conversation in a way that doesn't blame your teen***
Say something like this: "Well, I think we have accomplished a lot." (This is true even if all you have accomplished is exposing your own sin.) "I hope this will be a start to truly understanding your needs and struggles in ways that will build a good relationship between us. That's what I want, and I believe that is what you want. I hope you will give some thought to all we have talked about. Perhaps you will think of other things that will help me to be more effective. I welcome that. We will talk again in a few days about this—okay?

"Here is a passage to think about. Psalm 37 reminds us what is important. Listen to these words from the Psalmist."

> Trust in the LORD, and do good;
>     dwell in the land and befriend faithfulness.
> Delight yourself in the LORD,
>     and he will give you the desires of your heart.
> Commit your way to the LORD;
>     trust in him, and he will act.
> He will bring forth your righteousness as the light,
>     and your justice as the noonday.
> (Psalm 37:3–6)

"Let's pray and ask God to bless our efforts."

Be sure to thank your child for meeting with you. It may or may not be a good time to set a date for the next conversation. Be sensitive to your teen. Allow at least a couple of days to a week—this is heavy stuff for him to take in!

***Pray in your child's presence***
This is so important. You have been praying privately or with your spouse about this conversation. Your child needs to know that prayer has been an integral part of your journey. You are extending your personal prayer now to include your child.

Begin your prayer by repenting for your sins in relationship with your child. Pray confidently for your own change, humility, and growth because of Christ's enablement. Pray for your child's tenderness toward God and Christ, as well as your efforts to heal and reclaim your relationship. Pray that your family will be a beautiful shelter and growing place for ministry in Christ's kingdom for everyone in it, and a testimony to the watching world of the power of the gospel.

***Don't be discouraged***

It is impossible to script all the potential outcomes for a conversation such as this. It may disappoint your expectations. But remember, this conversation is to disarm your child's sense of justification against your parenting—which is how you got here to begin with—not to make you feel better or successful. Courage and dependence on Christ are essential. So is humility. Galatians 6:9 counsels us in these words: *And let us not grow weary of doing good, for in due season we will reap, if we do not give up.*

***Genuine relationship is more than discipline***

One last observation: One of the most common reasons for breakdown between Christian parents and children is this: The temptation for busy parents is to spend more time in conversation with children over discipline issues than for any other purpose! Children resent this. They feel like their parents' only interest in them is that they obey and look and act respectable so that their Christian home and witness will be well represented.

As you undertake this disarming process, relationship building is paramount! *Be sure* that you make big strides in spending time with your teens just talking about what they like, what they believe they're good at, what their plans and dreams are, whom they get along with, and what makes them happy, sad, scared, and mad. Welcome your teen to ask questions about the Christian faith and to share their misgivings and doubts. Don't respond with fear and gasping if they register doubts about faith. This is a necessary transition from accepting the Christian faith taught in your home to making it their own faith. Take them places, show them things you're interested in, thinking about, praying about. (Go easy on this or their eyes will glaze over with boredom!) You will be amazed that such efforts at genuine relationship-building with your teen, with no discipline or heavy agenda attached, will facilitate the disarming process. Be sure that you are making big strides in spending relationship-building time with your teen.

*Set a time for the next conversation*

Allow time for your child to process all that has been said. Also, talk with your spouse or a trusted adviser about your first encounter. Consider how you might have expressed things better so that you are prepared for the next conversation.

If you are thinking now, "You just don't know my teenager!", you're right. I don't. But God does. And he is able to make your humble obedience to his truth effective and productive in your home.

In all these efforts, you should, by God's grace, exhibit the fruit of the Spirit and the whole armor of God. Remember, this is not only about changing behavior. This is a spiritual endeavor—a holy mission. Be sure your own heart has known the care of the Master Gardener—that strong roots and good fruit are evident. Otherwise, your work will be in vain and you will reap harder hearts than before! Our hope is this: *"And a harvest of righteousness is sown in peace by those who make peace"* (James 3:18).

Where do you go from here? Continue to apply the same truth to future conversations. Prayer and reflection, the use of God's Word, and confidence in Christ will prepare you well for future conversations.

***When do I conclude that my young adult child should no longer stay in my home?***

There may come a time when your young adult child has made choices that mean he should not continue to live in your home. This would be true if your child is unwilling to maintain those biblical absolutes that shape family life and practice.

It is important to distinguish between personal preferences and moral/ethical issues dictated by the principles and absolutes of Scripture. For instance, your child may not dress in a style that is to your liking, but as long as it is not immoral, it should not be an issue. But behavior or appearance that breaks God's law or civil law creates compromise that you cannot countenance in your home. Issues such as substance abuse, sexual or gender related sin, larceny, felony and misdemeanors would fall into that category.

Parents are tempted to feel angry at their child and feel guilty themselves when "putting their child out" seems like the only solution to growing unrest in their home.

It is difficult and sad when parents and adult children reach such an impasse. But do not make the mistake of interpreting this as failure. Remember that God is not hindered in his work in people's hearts by the ups and downs of human interaction. The important issue for us is how we approach and respond to such crises in relationships with our children.

***Be Proactive***

When your teen finishes high school, it is a good time to have an important talk. Tell your teen that he is embarking on adult life. He will increasingly bear responsibility for his expenses and lifestyle. Identify areas where your expectations of him may be a change from his experience as an adolescent and/or high school student. He should already be accustomed to responsibilities such as laundry and household chores, or even paying some of his own expenses such as car insurance and fuel.

None of that changes if your young adult child is remaining in your home or even just spending college breaks with you. But often, young adults lose a sense of community when they believe that they are now their own decision makers. You can head this misconception off by tackling the matter before it becomes a problem. The danger is obvious if you don't. Your child begins to live as an independent person in your home and you begin to have a growing sense of frustration and hurt because he no longer behaves like a contributing member of the family. Your relationship deteriorates as you respond to him from your feeling of hurt and a growing sense of frustration. Your child begins to feel resentful of your disapproval, silent treatment, and anger. This devolves into a downward spiral of a disintegrating relationship.

***How can I disarm my adult child when I must also ask him to leave our home?***

What if the parent-child relationship is already broken? You have applied all the teaching of previous chapters, but your child remains unmoved. His unwillingness to cooperate with family life has left you believing that you must ask your young adult child to leave your home. How can you proceed without undoing all your efforts thus far to disarm him?

Your first conversation must be to establish the necessary expectations for your home. This includes the necessity to live responsibly in the family community as well as within the Christian boundaries described in Scripture. If this was done as described above, you are reminding your child of the things he agreed to. If this was not already done as described above, it should be lovingly and graciously covered as a first conversation with your child. Allow for questions and clarification to be sure all is understood. Ask your child to let you know whether he believes he is able to agree to and cooperate with those expectations. Make it clear that you are determined to talk openly and constructively when you have concerns for his cooperation. Welcome your child to bring issues up with you when he feels misunderstood or unfairly treated.

Assure your child of your understanding that he is an adult and has the right to make decisions. Your adult child has the responsibility and privilege of establishing his schedule and personal standards. But also clarify that, as a member of the family community, he must have the courtesy to let you know things such as schedule and plans so that you can manage family life appropriately.

When it becomes apparent that your child is either unable or unwilling to cooperate with the standards you have set for your home, here are suggestions for your conversation: "We love you and want what is best for you. We are committed to you and want to help you to be successful. At the same time, it is apparent to us, and we are sure it is to you, too, that we are at odds over issues of living together. As a matter of Christian conscience, we cannot change our standards, and you have made different decisions about your own standards. Do you know what we're talking about?" Give opportunity for your child to interact and agree or disagree with those statements. You may need to illustrate your diverging paths, but be careful to represent him accurately. Do not embellish for the sake of argument or use accusing or inflammatory words to describe him or his choices.

Then continue in words such as these: "We are open to trying to overcome these obstacles. But if we are not able to resolve these issues in ways that respect your choices and our choices, we believe that it is time for you to establish your own household. So, we have two conversations before us. The first—and the one we would prefer—is that we are able to come to agreement on how to live together in ways that allow us to maintain the Christian atmosphere of our home and also respect your place as an adult living in our home. The second option is how we can help and support you to be successful in launching into your own home. We want, with all our hearts, to have a relationship of mutual respect and love for one another. If you choose to live independently, we will do everything we can to facilitate your successful transition to your own home. What do you think about these options?" Allow for questions and both positive and negative responses. Be quick to say that you are opening a dialogue and make it clear that you are not looking for immediate decisions.

If your child responds, "I would love to leave, but I can't afford to live on my own," you could respond in this way: "We understand that this is a real obstacle to your desire for independence. Since that is the case, we can consider two things: First, while we are sympathetic to your dilemma, and we want to make every concession we are able to in good conscience, we cannot continue to have you live here unless you are willing to cooperate with our family standards. We must work these issues out and we are willing to undertake that discussion. Secondly, perhaps it is time for you to both consider how you can provide for yourself and to get needed help with budgeting and decision making that will facilitate your independence. We would be happy to help you with that or we can recommend trusted advisors who could help you with your goals."

Asking an adult child to leave home is often misunderstood as necessarily resulting in a broken relationship. However, if it is handled with Christian love and wisdom, it need not rupture your relationship. Again, this may take a series of conversations.

Remember that our purpose in conversations such as these with our children is not to drag them kicking and screaming to our destination. It is to bring them along with us with winsome and sound biblical reasoning.

> The heart of the wise makes his speech judicious
> and adds persuasiveness to his lips.
> (Proverbs 16:23)

# 9

# *What If All My Efforts to Disarm Rebellion Fail?*

"I tried your disarming process and it didn't work! I give up. I can't do this anymore! It hurts too much! I don't want to talk about it or think about it anymore!" What if your child continues in his rebellion even after you have toiled in the disarming process? What if he resists reconciliation? What if this rebellious child is now an adult who has fled your home, and your efforts seem too little too late?

Let me suggest a new way of looking at your experience. Rather than concluding that all your efforts have failed, you could remember God's promises and conclude, "It hasn't worked yet!" There are three reasons for this optimism.

FIRST, you are never at the place where your work has been in vain. You are on a journey. As long as your children are breathing, there is hope. Continue to love them, reach out to them, acknowledge your own sin with humility, and look for relationship-building opportunities. Don't give up when they reject your overtures or your invitations. Instead, send sweet, approving texts. Send pictures of your events and joys. Welcome theirs and make lavish comments about their accomplishments; and be sure to remember their special occasions.

Resist the temptation to make it about you! Don't say, "I can't bear to have a superficial relationship with people I love. I can't bear to not share family times." When you cave in to those thoughts, you isolate yourself to avoid pain. When you conclude that there is no hope or that you cannot bear any more, you have made this attempt at reconciliation all about yourself. In fact, you are no longer on a mission of love and reconciliation. You love yourself more than your children and you have made a lie of God's promises and of his model of reconciliation. Sometimes this means you can't have the relationship you long for. You may need to be content to have the relationship you *can have,* and work toward a better relationship.

This admonition may sound harsh to you and I understand why you would think so. But think about Philippians 2. Isn't that exactly the point?

> So if there is any encouragement in Christ, any comfort from love, any participation in the Spirit, any affection and sympathy, complete my joy by being of the same mind, having the same love, being in full accord and of one mind. Do nothing from selfish ambition or conceit, but in humility count others more significant than yourselves. Let each of you look not only to his own interests, but also to the interests of others. Have this mind among yourselves, which is yours in Christ Jesus, who, though he was in the form of God, did not count equality with God a thing to be grasped, but emptied himself, by taking the form of a servant, being born in the likeness of men. And being found in human form, he humbled himself by becoming obedient to the point of death, even death on a cross.
> (Philippians 2:1–8)

A summary of this passage might be: If you know Christ's love and all the attending blessings, you should have the same agenda Christ had in relationship to you. He considered you before himself even to laying down his life for you.

SECOND, success in the reconciliation process is not measured by results from your efforts. "Giving up" is a sign that you are hoping in your efforts rather than the work of God's Spirit. Remember the farming analogy we started with? We are the planters and waterers. He brings the harvest. When we grow weary of the disarming process, we need the encouragement of 1 Corinthians 3, where Paul is admonishing believers against mere hope in human efforts to produce spiritual results.

> What then is Apollos? What is Paul? Servants through whom you believed, as the Lord assigned to each. I planted, Apollos watered, but God gave the growth. So neither he who plants nor he who waters is anything, but only God who gives the growth. He who plants and he who waters are one, and each will receive his wages according to his labor. For we are God's fellow workers. You are God's field, God's building.
> (1 Corinthians 3:5–9)

So, we cannot take credit for results, because it is God who makes our efforts fruitful. In the same way, when we do not yet see fruit, we cannot conclude that our efforts are of no use, because it is God's work in God's time that brings the increase. Giving up is unbelief. Persevering is belief in God's promises.

Consider the following passages in light of your disappointment over your efforts to disarm your child.

Psalm 62 provides a wonderful model for responding to damaged relationships and personal attacks. David is responding to circumstances surrounding his son, Absalom, and the planned coup of Absalom and his followers to take the throne away from David.

> For God alone my soul waits in silence;
> from him comes my salvation.
> He alone is my rock and my salvation,
> my fortress; I shall not be greatly shaken.
> How long will all of you attack a man
> to batter him,
> like a leaning wall, a tottering fence?
> They only plan to thrust him down from his high position.
> They take pleasure in falsehood.
> They bless with their mouths,
> but inwardly they curse.
> (Psalm 62: 1–4)

David begins his response to the disloyalty and lies of his son and other enemies described in verses 3 and 4 with a statement of his theology—what he believes about God—in verses 1 and 2. His confidence, hope, and comfort are not in changed circumstances or even in the restoration of his relationship with his son. It is in God alone. That is what he believes to be true. He interprets the actions of people and circumstances of his life through the lens of the unseen world, through spiritual reality, out of which God rules and dispenses justice and comfort for his people. Rather than focusing on the hurt and injustice of his circumstances, he focuses on God's agenda for him. Notice that David doesn't make little of the grief he is facing. Rather, he is comparing the truth he believes about God with the drama of his circumstances. He concludes that God's provision and care are greater than his dilemma. So, first, he rehearses his theology, a sound place to plant his hurting soul.

In verses 5–8, David makes a critical transition from his theology to a very personal application.

> For God alone, O my soul, wait in silence,
> for my hope is from him.
> He only is my rock and my salvation,
> my fortress; I shall not be shaken.
> On God rests my salvation and my glory;
> my mighty rock, my refuge is God.
> Trust in him at all times, O people;
> pour out your heart before him;
> God is a refuge for us.
> (Psalm 62:5–8)

He stated his theological belief in verses 1–2. Out of that theology, he now speaks to his soul. He counsels his soul to find rest in that unseen world he believes exists. He takes his eyes away from his son and his enemies and places his eyes on God. We have a little window into his enthusiasm in this personal application of truth as it spills out into a plea for all people to pour out their hurting hearts to God—who is a refuge for his people. God is the shelter into which we can run when all else fails. He is a sufficient reference point for all the grief and tragedy of our lives. David gets it! He has made his theology personal. It reminds me of Psalm 34:18: *The* LORD *is near to the brokenhearted and saves the crushed in spirit.* There's a sense in which we all know the experience of pouring out our troubles to a trusted friend. That's what David is talking about. He has poured out his agony to God—he has unburdened his soul . . so there is nothing left bottled up inside his heart, and the godly sense of relief is seen in the remainder of the Psalm.

In verses 9–12, David cinches his determination to trust in God alone.

Those of low estate are but a breath;
    those of high estate are a delusion;
in the balances they go up;
    they are together lighter than a breath.
Put no trust in extortion;
    set no vain hopes on robbery;
    if riches increase, set not your heart on them.
Once God has spoken;
    twice have I heard this:
that power belongs to God,
    and that to you, O Lord, belongs steadfast love.
For you will render to a man
    according to his work.
(Psalm 62:9–12)

Nothing in this creation—whether status, privilege, stealth or wealth—can give us the hope and assurance we need to face the challenges of life. Perfect power and unfailing love are the exclusive properties of God and are sufficient to meet the challenges and disappointments we face. David concludes with confidence that God will bring the spiritual reward of rest and peace to all who put their hope in God.

David expresses through this powerful psalm a profound universal spiritual truth that allows us to live through deep circumstantial and relationship disappointments with hope—and even rest—for our souls. We are not okay because of people or circumstances, or because parents, spouses, children, co-workers, or life's circumstances are ideal or even tolerable. We are okay because we have in God and his provision of Christ all that we need.

A THIRD REASON for optimism is in God's agenda for us as parents.

God has an agenda for parents in all this—he is humbling you and making you like Christ. God's agenda for his people is to make them holy. He is always at work to refine us in our trials, whether they are trials of our making, or foisted on us by others or the circumstances of life.

C.H. Spurgeon has this most memorable thought about trials. He states: "I have learned to kiss the waves that throw me against the Rock of Ages." Embrace the trial because it takes you to God. His purpose is that you see his glory, his refiner's fire, his purpose to bring you out as pure gold. Don't think, "How can I fix my rebellious kid?" Think, rather, "How is God fixing me in this trial? How is he using people and circumstances to make me more like Christ, both for use in his kingdom now, and to glory in him for eternity?"

Often parents are caught up with what may be thought of as "plausible idols." We can easily identify the idols of the world: success, wealth, popularity, sensuality. But we are often blind to the good and desirable longings that become a god in our hearts. These are plausible idols. It is good and desirable to have our children live with loyalty and love for their parents. It is lovely to have the family grow in mutuality and service together for Christ's Kingdom. It is precious to see one generation follow another in God's ways, and we all want that for our family. The danger for us comes when we must have these results from our efforts as parents or we are disconsolate and in despair. We can find no comfort or hope in God when our longings are not met by children and family.

That's the point Paul makes so poignantly in 2 Corinthians 4, where he concludes in these words:

> So we do not lose heart. Though our outer self is wasting away, our inner self is being renewed day by day. For this light momentary affliction is preparing for us an eternal weight of glory beyond all comparison, as we look not to the things that are seen but to the things that are unseen. For the things that are seen are transient, but the things that are unseen are eternal.
> (2 Corinthians 4:16–18)

***Comparison again. . .***

God created us for relationships. Relationship is one of the image-of-God qualities we enjoy. Our vertical relationship with God and our horizontal relationships with others were patterned after the relationship of love, communication, and purpose present between God the Father, God the Son, and God the Holy Spirit. It is not surprising, then, that our hearts are broken by the loss of a relationship in God's most central human relationship circle, the family. But, praise God, he has not left us without hope in the face of the fall. He has created the means of reconciliation. The path of reconciliation is demonstrated through truth taught in his revelation and illustrated graphically and literally through the incarnation, life, death, and resurrection of the Lord Jesus Christ. The apostle Paul expressed it in these words:

> Therefore, knowing the fear of the Lord, we persuade others. But what we are is known to God, and I hope it is known also to your conscience. We are not commending ourselves to you again but giving you cause to boast about us, so that you may be able to answer those who boast about outward appearance and not about what is in the heart. For if we are beside ourselves, it is for God; if we are in our right mind, it is for you. For the love of Christ controls us, because we have concluded this: that one has died for all, therefore all have died; and he died for all, that those who live might no longer live for themselves but for him who for their sake died and was raised.
>
> From now on, therefore, we regard no one according to the flesh. Even though we once regarded Christ according to the flesh, we regard him thus no longer. Therefore, if anyone is in Christ, he is a new creation. The old has passed away; behold, the new has come. All this is from God, who through Christ reconciled us to himself and gave us the ministry of reconciliation; that is, in Christ God was reconciling the world to himself, not counting their trespasses against them, and entrusting to us the message of reconciliation. Therefore, we are ambassadors for Christ, God making his appeal through us. We implore you on behalf of Christ, be reconciled to God. For our sake he made him to be sin who knew no sin, so that in him we might become the righteousness of God.
>
> (2 Corinthians 5:11–21)

I am not denying the heartache and sense of loss that attends broken relationships with children, but despair is the product of unbelief. We must remind ourselves that it is God's Spirit who brings change—not our efforts.

What can you do? Continue to follow God's direction for living a life of genuine and humble Christian faith before your children. Love your rebellious child as God loved you. Surround all your expectations with the beauty, grace, compassion, and understanding that Christ offered to you in his perfect life and death on your behalf. Remember, Christ is still making intercession on your behalf before the Father. Your rebellious child should see in your face and hear in your voice the same welcome that Christ extends to all who are in peril.

If you find yourself in despair, don't lose heart. Remember Christ's call recorded in Matthew 11. This is not only a call to the unbeliever to repent and believe; it is also the shelter for the weary and struggling believer's soul.

> Come to me, all who labor and are heavy laden, and I will give you rest. Take my yoke upon you, and learn from me, for I am gentle and lowly in heart, and you will find rest for your souls. For my yoke is easy, and my burden is light. (Matthew 11:28–30)

I know this feels like hard teaching. It is hard to humble ourselves to acknowledge our complicity in broken relationships. It is hard to repent without defending even our just and honorable sacrifice, our good intentions, and sincere efforts as parents. It is hard to confront rebellion with Christlike attitudes. How can we do this disarming ministry? Peter provides a timely reminder for our guidance and encouragement.

> His divine power has granted to us all things that pertain to life and godliness, through the knowledge of him who called us to his own glory and excellence, by which he has granted to us his precious and very great promises, so that through them you may become partakers of the divine

nature, having escaped from the corruption that is in the world because of sinful desire.
(2 Peter 1:3–4)

*Shepherding a Child's Heart*
*Tedd Tripp*
*Paperback, 214 pages*
*ISBN 9780966378603*

*Shepherding a Child's Heart* is about how to speak to the heart of your child. The things your child does and says flow from the heart. Luke 6:45 puts it this way: "...out of the overflow of the heart the mouth speaks." Written for parents with children of any age, this insightful book provides perspectives and procedures for shepherding your child's heart into the paths of life.

In this revised edition of *Shepherding a Child's Heart*, Dr. Tedd Tripp not only draws on his thirty years experience as a pastor, counselor, school administrator, and father, but he also shares insights gained in many years of teaching this material in conferences worldwide, providing more valuable help for parents.

"This is a masterful book."
—Dr. David Powlison, Westminster Theological Seminary

"Tedd Tripp offers solid, trustworthy, biblical help for parents. If you are looking for the right perspective and practical help, you won't find a more excellent guide."
—John MacArthur

"Dr. Tripp's material on parenting is the clearest, most biblically framed, and most helpful that I have ever encountered."
—Dr. Edward Welch, Christian Counseling and Educational Foundation

*Instructing a Child's Heart*
*Tedd and Margy Tripp*
*Paperback, 188 pages*
*ISBN 9780981540009*

This book provides a crucial foundation for the principles in *Shepherding a Child's Heart*, teaching parents the importance of developing and shaping their children's thinking. This formative instruction is not discipline or correction; rather, it is intentionally building a biblical culture of thought and understanding in our homes.

*Instructing a Child's Heart* is an essential "how-to" manual for Shepherding a Child's Heart, helping parents provide their children with a biblical framework for approaching and understanding all of life.

> "Biblical. Practical. Pastoral. This insightful book on godly childrearing is everything we would expect from the author who brought us Shepherding a Child's Heart. Its tremendous value comes from the fact that it centers on the essential but oft-neglected heart of biblical parenting: the Gospel of grace. I am glad to recommend it."
> —John MacArthur

> "A biblical and practical sequel to Shepherding a Child's Heart."
> —Marvin Olasky, World Magazine

***About Shepherd Press Publications***

*They are gospel driven.*
*They are heart focused.*
*They are life changing.*

***Our Invitation to You***

We passionately believe that what we are publishing can be of benefit to you, your family, your friends, and your work colleagues. So we are inviting you to join our online mailing list so that we may reach out to you with news about our latest and forthcoming publications, and with special offers.

Visit:

www.shepherdpress.com/newsletter

and provide your name and email address.